.25

Contemporary
Pastoral Prayers
for the
Christian Year

Contemporary Pastoral Prayers for the Christian Year

by
Nathanael M. Guptill

CHRISTIAN EDUCATION PRESS

PHILADELPHIA

Contents

Preface

The newspaper reporter has his deadline. The matador has his "moment of truth." The pastor has those two weekly entries on the order of worship, "Sermon" and "Pastoral Prayer." Most of us, after a good deal of agony and not a little experimentation, settle down to a habitual pattern of preparation that is kindest to one particular set of weaknesses. For reasons I am not prepared to defend by any logic, my custom is to preach without notes and to read, or memorize, my prayers. This is why my first book of prayers precedes my first book of sermons. (In fact, the world may well be spared the latter discipline.)

This book suggests a method of preparation and delivery and a set of prayers for every Sunday of the year. The method is not original. Every pastor is drawn, at one time or another, to four basic styles of pastoral prayer. There is the impromptu method which involves no preparation save the composing of the minister's own spirit. There is the extempore method in which an outline or sequence of thought is either brought into the pulpit or committed to memory in advance. There is the method of using prayers written by the minister himself, and finally, there is the prayer-book method using the formal prayers printed in liturgical manuals.

It need hardly be said that these methods may be combined in an infinite variety of ways. Each method has its own set of advantages and disadvantages. The only real heresy is to state dogmatically that any one pattern is always better than the others.

For instance, an increase of pious fervor often accompanies impromptu prayer. For the years when I was experimenting with different kinds of pastoral prayers I remember a faithful parishioner who preferred the impromptu or extempore to the read prayers. She claimed that she could tell without looking whether I was reading or not, confessing that she verified her theory by peeking in the middle once in a while. How much of the increased intensity is due to the closer presence of the Spirit and how much to empathy with the minister as he stumbles and fumbles in search of words would be difficult to determine. Certainly the impromptu prayer takes more out of the preacher during the service; while the written prayer takes more out of him in his hours of preparation during the week.

A long time ago in George A. Buttrick's book entitled *Prayer* I read his suggestion that a series of short prayers is to be preferred to a single long prayer, the intervening Amens having the effect of reassembling the woolgatherers periodically. While this is a sad commentary on the attention span of the average congregation, I am inclined to think it is true; therefore my order of worship includes pastoral prayers rather than a pastoral prayer, and the prayers in this book are cast in triple or quadruple form. Each of the prayers on a given page may be concluded, as in my own practice, with some such appropriate phrase as "through Jesus Christ our Lord."

Whatever method a minister finally settles upon for his own, or even if he never settles but continues to vary his practice all his life, it is certain that the discipline of reading and writing prayers is a good one. It is possible, of course, for one to read and write prayers without praying, a talent not to be cultivated. If, in this exercise, one remembers to set his soul in a Godward direction, it cannot but bless him and his congregation.

The prayers that appear here were written under the awful urgency of preparing for the Sunday service. They have been prayed in church. I share them with my fellow ministers for whatever use they may desire to make of them.

I hope this book will prime the pumps of the imagination. I would not object if, some weeks when the sermon comes hard and there is not time to prepare the prayers, these prayers should be prayed again in church. The rules of proprietorship are not the same with prayers as with sermons.

NATHANAEL M. GUPTILL

G*racious God,* unstop the ears of our souls that we may hear thy voice speaking to us the words we need to hear. Daily we are deafened by the clamor of this world's voices, the radio and the press with their shouts of greed and despair, the evil persuasions that rise from within ourselves, fear and pride and selfish prejudice. Thy words are drowned out in the endless clatter and traffic of our mechanistic civilization. But here in this house it is not so. This is thy house, built to thy glory by loving hands. Here for many years thy children have come to worship and gone forth to the labors of thy kingdom. Thy voice is here and we wait expectantly in thy presence.

Speak to us from the cross that stands before us. Speak to us from the holy book whose pages tell of thy blessed invasion of human history. Speak to us in the songs of devotion passed down to us from men of old. Speak in the fellowship whereby in silence we pray together or in common phrases we declare our faith in thee. Create in us clean hearts, O God, and renew a right spirit within us. Help us to know that thou art our Father, loving and wise and almighty, that we can safely make thy will our will and trust thee for all that is to come until the day breaks and the shadows flee away.

Having lifted our lives from the depths to the heights send us forth, O God, upon thine errands. Grant that we may be thy people, the good friends of all holy labor and the foes of all corruption and evil in places high or low. May our fears and problems be drowned in a mighty concern for the ongoing of thy kingdom, and our lives made whole in the service of the Master, for we pray in his holy name. Amen.

2

O *God Most High* who with glorious condescension dost abide in the heart that truly seeks thee, come and be with us met together in this thy house. Let this hour be a pilgrimage to the holy of holies. Teach us that thy holy place is not a building or any earthly city but a corner of the human heart that loves thee. Come to our hearts and abide. Thou art so great and we are so insignificant that we cannot possibly know thee fully as thou art, but we thank thee that thou hast sent us thy Son, Jesus, to be thine ambassador and our High Priest. Draw us in this hour close to him that he may bring us close to thee.

Help us by being good friends of Christ to apprehend his living spirit. Bring him out of the Book alive, so that not through dogma and precept but through the kindling touch of another soul we may be set alight with the love that is from on high. Fill our lives with that creative compassion of Christ that comes to us from thee through him. Let it crowd out of our spirits all selfish fear and anxiety, filling us full of the desire to think and do those things that shall work to the establishment of thy kingdom.

We have tried, O God, to save our lives, to hoard our hours and our goods unto ourselves; but we have found the truth of the saying that whosoever would have his life shall lose it, we have seen that the selfishness by which we sought to live leads only to death; so now we would commit our lives to thee completely, confident that what we love is safer in thy hands than in ours. Help us confidently to spend our lives unstintingly with Christ who spent his life for us, that true goodness may abound among thy people both here and everywhere. Hear us, O God, for we pray in Jesus' name. Amen.

A *lmighty* *and* *eternal* *God,* whom to worship is to know, whom to know is to love, and whom to love is to serve, we come to thee this day according to our custom to set in motion in our lives the spiritual powers of worship and knowledge and love and service. Help us, we pray thee, to worship thee in spirit and in truth. Let us bow before thee not only our heads but also our hearts. Breathe upon us thy Holy Spirit until we are still and know that thou art God. And knowing thee who art eternal love, may the drought in our spirits be ended, and may there well up within us, filling the parched pools of our lives with living water, an overflowing measure of thine own grace, crowding out our pride and hatred, transforming our weakness into power from thee for service in thy name.

O thou Author of liberty, as our souls cry out for freedom from the shackles that enslave us, do thou teach us the true liberty of willing obedience to thy holy will. Help us so to desire the thing that thou commandest that thy will may be our will, and that our fellowship together and with thee may be one of perfect freedom. Take the desires and petitions of our hearts and grant such as may be most expedient for us, according to thy gracious promises.

Hear us, O God, as we pray for one another and for thy people everywhere. Sustain our faith, increase our hope and love, that the day may be hastened when thy kingdom shall come, thy will be done on earth as it is in heaven, through Jesus Christ our Lord. Amen.

O *God,* since we cannot see thee with the eye of flesh we thank thee for the eyes of faith whereby men have beheld thy glory in all the ages. We bless thy name for those in every generation who have laid hold on thee steadfastly and in the midst of doubt and turmoil have found the joy and peace that comes with believing. We thank thee for Abraham of old and for all other men of faith who have followed in his train, especially for good parents and teachers and friends who have quickened in our own minds the heavenly vision. Let this service of worship, we pray thee, strengthen the faith by which we live and deepen the loyalty that binds our lives to each other and to thee.

Let the importance of our mission as members of thy church in the world be borne in upon us. Weak are we and sinful, not worthy to carry thy standard in a world like this. Yet thou art able to use even our weakness to magnify thy power. Strengthen our hands and enable us in word and deed to lift the cross of Christ on high that all may see.

We know, O Lord, that we fall short of being real Christians, that we miss the glow of real grace and the powerful life that is the mark of the saints. Break down that last barrier of selfish concern that separates us from thee and let our lives be flooded by thy Spirit. Wash away the accumulated dross of fear and grief and greed that our souls may be clean again. Renew our fading zeal that we may go forth and labor with a will in that corner of thy domain which thou callest us to tend. And to thee be all the glory, world without end, in Christ our Lord. Amen.

O thou almighty God who also art our Father, be with us as we keep our tryst with thee in thy house. We gratefully remember before thee the people who in days gone by have come to this place to praise thee and seek thy help. We rejoice that thou didst guide them by the same Spirit that quickens our hearts today. Make us conscious of the human chain of which we are a part, a chain that reaches back to Jesus and around the world, and renew our sense of the power of that holy mingling of spirits.

We thank thee, O God, for all special benefits thou hast heaped upon us above all other peoples: for the order and abundance and freedom of our country, for the homely blessings of friends and folks, and for all the little things we take for granted every day. Thou hast made us, and not we ourselves. For the good gift of life we give thee thanks.

O heavenly Father, as children bring their problems to their wise and loving parents, so we bring our problems to thee this day. Worries we have about our daily tasks, lest they be left unfinished or done not well. Anxieties we have about ourselves and those we love, lest we fall into danger or misfortune or pain. Fears we have of thy judgment upon our sins both known and unknown, for in many ways and on many days we have fallen short by far of thy purpose for us. We here offer ourselves to thee wholly. We confess that we know not how to live apart from thee. Take us to be thine, and let all our worries and anxieties and fears be melted in the warmth of thy grace. Send us forth from this place refreshed and strong and glad to be this week neither fearful nor defeated but as those who walk with assurance because they walk with God. Hear these and all our prayers in the name of Jesus, the Prince of Life. Amen.

O *God, our Father,* we thank thee for the matchless privilege of prayer. Finite creatures, imprisoned in time and space, we can, nevertheless, reach out through the veil of flesh and lay hold on eternity by the prayers of faith. Remembering thy promise that wherever two or three are gathered together in thy name there thou art in the midst, we have knowledge that this our fellowship is holy with nearness to thee. Let our worship be full of the powerful grace of thy Spirit, and all our days be better for it.

We remember in thy presence all children of thine who have special need of thy merciful care. We pray for the sick and the aged, that they may be comforted and that thy love may be in those who care for them. We pray for the leaders of our nation and for all others in positions of high authority; teach them the hard lesson that those who would be great must be the servants of all. We pray for students and for all young people, that in their preparations for life they may not neglect the nurture of the spirit but may grow in wisdom and purity as well as in stature. We pray for one another, that nobody may leave this place without a glimpse of thy beauty, a sense of thy forgiveness, a supply of thy grace sufficient for the week.

Increase, O Lord, the bonds that bind men together in sympathy and understanding. Confound the labors of those who would peddle hatred among races, classes, and nations. Increase the strength of all who labor for thy kingdom of peace. And to thee be the glory, in Christ Jesus our Lord. Amen.

O God, who dost paint the bright blue sky of autumn, who bringest the light out of darkness, and from whom cometh every good and perfect gift, we are overcome with gratitude for the precious right to worship. Thanksgiving wells up in our hearts and overflows in hymns of praise. For all that makes life worth the living we thank thee.

O thou who art the Ruler of all the nations, we pray for this our native land. Let our bounty be sanctified by sharing, our power by right and generous use, and our learning by wisdom from on high. Be close to those who hold the reins of authority, that their decisions may be honorable because their hearts are open to the calling of thy Spirit.

O thou who art the Father of all mankind, we remember in thy presence all those who have been forgotten by their fellows: the aged and those who are lonely, the sick, the homeless children of the world, soldiers on faraway fields of battle, and all others who do not even come to our minds, but are still unforgotten by thee; grant unto them the sure knowledge that thou art by their side. Enfold them in thine everlasting arms. And renew the flagging zeal of thy church that a day may dawn when no one shall be forgotten or left out.

O God, we pray for one another met here in holy comradeship. May the love we receive from thee be increased in sharing, that being weak we may become strong because we have been together in thee. Let no one who here has offered himself to thee in worship go away empty and forlorn. Let no one who is proud go away without having his pride brought low before the cross. And because we have worshiped may our homes, our community, our nation, our world be more like thy kingdom, for whose coming we earnestly pray, in Jesus' holy name. Amen.

8

O eternal God, who wert in the beginning, art now, and ever shalt be the ruler and guardian of all thou hast made, we gather to praise thy name and to seek thy Spirit. We remember once again the unspeakable wonder of thy creation. We thank thee for this world balanced in the midst of space, so full of treasures for our taking: oil and coal and iron in the depths of the earth, the good soil from which soon we will gather the abundant harvest, the sun for our warmth and the bracing wind that fills our lungs with life. All these are thy creations; all are thy gifts of which we are unworthy.

We acknowledge this day, O Lord, that since thou hast made us we are thine; that we do not belong to ourselves but to thee. Repair the damage sin has wrought and refashion us anew according to the eternal pattern of Christ. Tear out from our souls all hate and lust and greed, and fill us with holy love whereby we may worship thee not only with our lips but in our lives. As the good carpenter takes a broken chair and smooths its rough places and mends its splintered parts, so do thou take us in thy hands once more and make us whole.

We thank thee for thy holy church by which we are ushered into thy presence, and we bless thy name for her world-wide mission of hope and peace. So bind us together with bonds of Christian fellowship that we, in the months that are ahead, may fulfill our share of that mission as good workmen of thine. Help us, each one, to walk among our brother men as those who have been in thy presence and received the blessing of thy gracious benediction. Let the light thou dost kindle in us here in this place so shine that many may glorify thee, for we pray in his name who is the Light of the world. Amen.

9

O *God of peace,* who speakest to mankind not in the wind or earthquake or fire, but in the voice of gentle stillness in the heart, we thank thee for the serenity that abides in thy presence. From the hectic hurly-burly of everyday life we come, full of discord and tumult, to thy house. We come to hear thy voice saying to the surging fears and wants of our minds what Jesus said to the waves of Galilee, "Peace, be still!" Quell our feverish longings with the knowledge that thou art all we need. Dispel our fears with the awareness that if thou art for us none can prevail against us. Lift us up above the confusing, crowded way of our lives until we can see the beginning and the ending in thee.

O God of hosts, having comforted us by thy peace do not let us rest in complacency, but send us forth when this hour is done as good soldiers of thine. Since by the healing of worship our lives are whole again let us go to battle against the powers of evil in our lives and in the world. May we be the enemies of falsehood and injustice, of prejudice and pride and greed whereever they appear. May we do battle as those who strive under a leader who has never been overthrown, with confidence and with poise. And may we have joy in the knowledge that even though we be defeated the cause for which we contend cannot be stayed and our defeat will become for us a victory even as the cross of Christ became his victory.

O God of love, whose compassion toward us is so great that thou didst send us thine only Son for our salvation, we adore thee because thou hast first loved us. Let this church we have established for thy glory be a proving ground in this world for that same holy love whereby we and our world must be saved, even the blessed love of Christ. Amen.

Eternal God, our Creator and our Destiny, thou who knowest us better than we know ourselves, draw near to us. Rekindle the flickering flames of faith within our cold lives that they may become warm again. Teach us by thy Spirit and by thy Word how to have courage and gladness in the midst of this world's shadows. And draw us this hour into the holy, healing fellowship of the church triumphant.

O thou great Judge of the nations, hear us as we pray this day for the United States of America, our native land. Teach our leaders, we beseech thee, that our nation can be strong only in thy strength. We thank thee for the ideal set up for us of one nation, indivisible, with liberty and justice for all. Forgive us that we have not lived up to this ideal. Increase our unity and our liberty and our justice. Let the people of Christ dare to speak and to act that thy voice may be heard and thy power may be revealed in this land we love.

We remember before thee this day all those here and elsewhere who have special need of thy grace, O God. Be very near to all who suffer, to the poor, the cold, and those enslaved by evil men or evil habits. By thy glorious gospel of hope, and by the power of faith, strike off the chains that bind men's souls. Let our prayers reach out to the indifferent and the lazy, the cruel and the selfish, that the good stuff of life thou hast created may not be wasted. And when we find ourselves in their number arouse us once again by the calling of him who said, "Follow me!" Let us begin this day to save the world where we can begin—by cleansing our own lives and giving them to thee. Here we are, Father, send us! We pray in Jesus' holy name. Amen.

A lmighty God, thou Creator and King of the universe, thy majesty is proclaimed by all thy creatures. The hills and the seas and the broad plains speak of thy grandeur. Birds and flowers and trees in many colors show forth thy beauty. Yet nowhere is thy glory made manifest as in the life of Jesus, thy Son. Above all earthly things, he stands as the link between earth and heaven, for he hath taught us to pray.

O Lord, who hast drawn us together as a church and hast bidden us love one another as thou hast loved us, we pray for all who belong to us and to whom we belong in this household of faith. We pray for those who serve as missionaries at outposts of thy kingdom. We remember those who wear the uniform of their country's service and walk in paths fraught with danger and temptation. We intercede for those who cannot worship in this place because of infirmity of body or soul. And we pray for one another as we with one voice sing thy praise and with one mind reaffirm our inward vows.

O heavenly Father, as we worship we are made aware of the many ways in which we have fallen short of the stature of Christ our goal and guide. We confess that good intentions we have expressed many times in this place have remained only intentions, and we are all too often meaner than we are noble. O God, forgive us, and renew a right spirit within us.

O God, who by thy Son Jesus Christ hast promised to the faithful that the deeds he did they can do and greater, stir up within us a great impatience with all halfheartedness and with all easy compromises, that our lives being empowered by a sure faith in thee and being directed by a clear knowledge of the gospel, may take on the radiance of his life in whose name we pray. Amen.

O *almighty God,* before whose face the centuries rise and pass away, we come to thee with awe and reverence. All that we see is mortal and changing. The green trees have become red and gold and soon their arms will stand bare against the sky. Nothing we know is permanent save thee alone. From everlasting to everlasting thou art God. We turn from the crumbling gods of earth and put our trust in thee.

We pray this day for all those in authority in our world: for thy servant the President of the United States, for the leaders of the United Nations, and for all other men and women who hold in their hands the guidance of thy people. Grant unto them the gift of spiritual vision, we pray thee, that they may find in obedience to thee the right ways wherein to lead us.

Our hearts go out in Christian love, O Lord, to all those who suffer for righteousness' sake. We remember before thee all missionaries in difficult stations, all laborers for truth and faith and freedom who are in danger because of their loyalty to thee. Be thou their strong Defender in all hardship, keeping them true to their calling in every testing.

As we come to thee in this service of worship, O God, come thou to meet us. Descend upon us with that peace which passeth understanding. Crowd out of our lives all fear, all suspicion, all malice, all doubt, and bestow upon us the knowledge that we are indeed in thy house. Let the strength of the saints of all the ages be ours as we join them in holy togetherness, and may the seeds of worship sown this day bear fruit in us unto good deeds for thy kingdom; through Jesus Christ our Lord. Amen.

O *God, our Governor and our Creator,* as the heavens are high above the earth so are thy ways high above our ways. Thou knowest us better than we know ourselves. Our lives are in thy hands. Here in thy house we acknowledge thee to be the Lord. As we are thy people be thou our God, we pray.

For all the days of our lives that we have known to be good we thank thee: for the dear ties of home and loved ones, for victories small and great thou hast given us to win, for tasks done, for friends made, for all thy good gifts we give thee praise. Grant that in days that are hard and times that are bad we may not forget thy past mercies. Keep us mindful that even in the darkest day thou art still loving us and canst convert despair to minister to our salvation. Take our hands in thy hand and lead us where thou wilt; only stay close to us when danger threatens and we are safe in thy care.

We bless thee for this holy miracle of prayer whereby, though separated by miles and oceans, we can reach out and touch each other through thy healing Spirit. We pray this day for all thy children, especially for those who have particular need of thy comfort. For the teeming millions of Asia facing another winter's cold and hunger with little hope, for the sick, the suffering, the aged, and the lonely wherever they may be, be thou a strong deliverer by thy judgment and thy love.

Let this hour of worship, we pray thee, be another turning point in our lives in which we fix our wills more steadfastly upon thy purpose for us, opening our minds to thy truth, storing up more of thy power in our hearts, and setting our feet firmly upon the way everlasting; through him who is the Way, the Truth, and the Life, Jesus our Lord. Amen.

1

Rally Day

O Lord, our God, on this day we pray for all church schools and especially for the one which gathers weekly in this house. We thank thee that there are men and women and young people who willingly give time and energy to this holy cause, and we pray that in thy mercy thou wilt increase their number, their wisdom, their strength, and their love for their pupils.

Do thou dwell mightily in the homes of this parish. Kindle once more the cold altars of family devotion. Teach us parents that the nurture of our children's souls is far more important than the training of their bodies and minds. If our time and strength are so small that we must neglect some phase of life let it not be the life of the Spirit.

We reach out hands of prayer to enfold all the children of the world: those running wild upon the streets of our cities, those who suffer the privation of over-devoted parents, those who are hungry in body and soul, and those who are born into a race regarded as second class. Increase human generosity by thy love that the hands of those who would rescue the lost among thy little ones may be strengthened. And renew in the mind of youth, O Lord, the sense of respect and gratitude, that those who have had opportunities for security and learning above the average may dedicate those gifts to the highest usefulness.

Above all, help us in thy holy church to keep open the channels of thy grace whereby old and young are drawn together in the fellowship of those who are committed to Christ. Let the church be his living body in the world to the end that not one of thy children shall perish. We pray in Jesus' name. Amen.

2

Rally Day

O *God,* we thank thee for the hour of worship. Lift our eyes from the streets to the skies. Lift our hearts with the joy of common praise. Acquaint us anew with the wonder that comes when we realize that the Ruler of the universe dwells in our midst. Let the clean air of holy togetherness with thee cleanse and refresh our souls.

Lord, on this day when our church is thronged again with young folks and little people and their elders, we remember before thee all those who are teachers. Remind them, we pray, that Jesus was not ashamed to be called Teacher. Let them know how holy a thing it is to impart to thy children the truth that makes men free. Let all who teach, whether in schools public or private, or as volunteers in the Sunday schools of our land, be endowed with holy wisdom that the lessons of eternal life may be taught and learned.

O God, we pray for the homes of this parish where children are growing up. Be near to all parents. Make them as eager to provide for the souls of their children as they are to provide for their bodies. Give them an abundance of the gifts so essential for parents: moral uprightness, patience, and love. Dwell in all Christian homes by thy Holy Spirit and make them outposts of thy kingdom, colonies of heaven.

Our Father, be close to each one of us in this hour. Thou knowest what we have need of before we ask it. Answer the prayers of thy people as may be best for them, and those things for which we ought to pray but know not how, do thou bestow in thy mercy. Enable us all, each at his own post, to be good workmen of thine, laborers for the coming of thy kingdom. Hear us, O Lord, for we pray in Jesus' name. Amen.

1

World-wide Communion

O *thou Great Spirit* who didst brood over the chaos and make out of it an orderly universe, we come to thee that thou mayest make order and harmony out of our chaotic lives. With us all things are temporary and passing; with thee is eternity. Give us a glimpse of things eternal, that we may know how our lives fit the everlasting pattern of thy kingdom.

We thank thee, O Lord, for this World-wide Communion Sunday. Today as on no other day we feel the kinship deeper than blood brotherhood that binds us to all others in the world who call upon the name of Christ. It is marvelous to us that that little fellowship of the upper room is now a great body of millions in every land under the sun. Let the bread and the cup offered throughout the world this day be received as from his own pierced hands, and in receiving these symbols into our bodies grant that we may truly receive him into our souls.

We pray, O God, for thy poor, blind, suffering world. We thank thee for what peace there is, and for the great fear of war that is in all human hearts. To that fear add, we pray thee, a willingness to pay the price of wholehearted devotion and obedience to thee which alone can buy lasting peace. And quicken thy church that she may speak so as to be understood and heeded by all the peoples of earth.

Begin with us, O Father. Our gifts are not great, but we offer them willingly to thee. Our gifts are as alike and as different as we, but receive them, O God, as thou didst receive the gift of Jesus—for the salvation of mankind and the coming of thy kingdom. Hear us, O Lord, for we pray in his holy name. Amen.

2
World-wide Communion

O God, who by thy Son Jesus Christ hast called men together in the blessed fellowship of the church, we thank thee this day for our membership in that company of the faithful of all times and all lands. Make known to us this hour how great a body it is of which we are a part, for we join with people white and black, yellow and brown, young and old, men and women and little children, in celebrating the central sacrament of our common faith, even the Supper of our Lord. In this hour may our hearts be knit one to another in bonds of mutual love, and may the hope we share in thee so fill our hearts that they will overflow abundantly in words and deeds of faith.

We remember before thee those in our fellowship around the world this day who are hungry and cold, those who gather in meetinghouses with thatched roofs or no roofs at all save the blue sky above, those with no shoes on their feet; and those with broken homes and broken hearts. Feed us all alike with thy sustaining grace, giving to the sorrowing, comfort; to the downtrodden, courage and hope; to the weak, might by thy Spirit; and to those more blest with peace and plenty, the added blessing of a compassionate heart.

We thank thee in this time of crisis that there are ties of Christian brotherhood stretching across oceans and continents, across man-made barriers of race and nation and class, maintaining even in the midst of hostility an association of holy friendship that reaches over the whole earth. Fill the empty reservoirs of our lives with living water, we pray thee, and send us forth upon thine errands, unto the salvation of our souls and the coming of thy kingdom, through Christ Jesus our Lord. Amen.

World-wide Communion

A lmighty God, we lift up our hearts to join in the chain of adoration which reaches around the world this day. In every language men adore thee. The chorus of the living blends with the heavenly choir of angels, prophets, apostles, saints, and martyrs of all ages, evermore lauding thee and saying, "Holy, holy, holy art thou, O God, the Father Eternal."

O Lord, we thank thee that thou hast called us to be one with the glorious company of thy people. Grant, we beseech thee, that our prayers for the rest of thy church going out from this place may meet other prayers for us and form a holy interlacing, binding us into one body, even the Body of Christ. We thank thee for the other churches of our community, for those whose spires dot the continents of the earth, especially for those little groups which meet in secret in China and Spain and other places where oppression reigns, and for every missionary who holds aloft the light of faith.

O thou great Judge of all the intentions of the heart, when we consider how great a sacrifice some have made for thy kingdom and how puny and halfhearted our devotion is, we are filled with sorrow and shame. Grant us the grace of true repentance, that our lives in home and office, in shop and community and church, may be more wholly devoted unto thee.

O living God, who of thy great mercy dost grant us the great privilege of worship, may this hour spent in thy presence purify and strengthen us body and soul. As we receive the sacrament of Christ's death may he come to life more and more in this, his church, to the end that thy love may be known among us. We offer all our prayers in Jesus' holy name. Amen.

1
Veterans' Day

A *lmighty God*, our Father and our King, we draw nigh unto
thee in this hour to blend our voices and our lives in the
eternal hymn of praise. Together with the blazing sun, the
roaring tempest, the choirs of angels and archangels and all the
chorus of creation we unite saying, "Holy, holy, holy, Lord,
God of Hosts. Heaven and earth are full of thy glory. Glory
be to thee, O Lord Most High!"

In this week when we recall the end of a great world war, we
note with shame that though many years have passed the hands
of man are still wet with the blood of his brother man. The
flying chariots of war still fill the air with thundering hate, and
whole generations of youth must learn anew the devilish art
of killing. O God, cleanse us, and fill us with a new passion for
peace more powerful than our passion for war. Let the living
energies of mankind be poured out for healing instead of harm-
ing, for life instead of death.

O tender Father of all mankind, we thank thee for the countless gifts of thy bounty: food and shelter in the midst of a world
hungry and cold; the privileges of freedom in a world half enslaved; family and friends to love and by whom to be loved;
work to do and truth to learn; and above all for the unspeakable
gift of thy Son.

On other days, O God, our souls are calloused and earth-
bound. But today our hearts are uplifted, our eyes are opened,
our hands are lifted in prayer. Seize us, O God, by our prayers
and make us thine. Clasp us to thyself that we may never again
be separated from thee, but walk in thy company every hour.
We pray in Jesus' holy name. Amen.

2

Veterans' Day

O living God who didst speak to Moses upon the holy mountain, who in the midst of the night didst call the child Samuel from his sleep, who didst reveal thyself to Isaiah with glory in the temple, thou Great Spirit in whom we live and move and have our being, come to us in this latter day as we wait in thy presence. Let the warning voice of conscience and the heartening voice of faith be heard in this place in this hour.

O great Lord, God of hosts, we pray for all soldiers and sailors as we remember the millions who have been enlisted in the service of their country to fight in wars not of their making. Especially do we offer up to thee in prayer those maimed and handicapped by injuries to body and mind, and the widows and the fatherless bereft of those who have died in battle. Grant, O Lord, that they may not be forgotten, and that the vast sacrifices of life may not have been in vain. May the hard lessons of war spur us on to find the ways of peace and to walk therein.

O God of the world-wide church, we pray for our church, the one we love the most. We thank thee for the beauty of this house of worship. We bless thy name for the holy friendships made here. Most of all we praise thee for Jesus Christ, our Elder Brother and our Lord. May the beauty and the power of his life permeate our associations until we are possessed completely by him. So may this church become an open doorway for the entry of thy Holy Spirit into the world. Hear this and all our prayers, for we offer them in Jesus' holy name. Amen.

1

World Order Day

O thou mighty God, by whom we were created, in whom we live and move and have our being, and unto whom we go when the labor of the day is past, we praise thee for the wondrous ordinance of worship whereby thy Spirit may gain entrance to our souls. We bless thy name that daily thou art with us, every hour more ready to listen than we are to pray. Especially do we thank thee for this hour when in the holy fellowship of thy church, world-wide and eternal, we may receive the power of thy love.

As always when we gather we bring thee, O Lord, our various needs. Some of us have grievous sins which need thy forgiveness, some have broken hearts that need binding up, and all of us have undeserved gifts from thee for which to offer thanks. Give us of thy mercy as may be best for us, and let no one go empty away. Empower us to give unto thee true repentance, true gratitude, true and complete dedication of that which we have to thy service.

In this autumn season when, in times past, it has been the horrible custom of man to begin his orgies of war, and also to begin his efforts for peace, we pray that the day of permanent peace amongst the nations may be hastened. Grant unto thy servants who represent the United Nations not only wisdom, but also patience and high resolve, so that the great desire of all the people of the world for peace may not be thwarted by the low machinations of those in high places.

And forbid it, Lord, that any should worship thee and go away as he came. Open our minds to receive thy truth and our hearts to receive thy love; set our wills alight with devotion that we may go forth to do thy will; through Jesus Christ our Lord. Amen.

2

World Order Day

O God, how great and terrible and holy a thing it is to bow in prayer to thee. It is to be a pygmy standing at the foot of a towering tree. It is to be dirty in the midst of a world pure white with new-fallen snow. It is to be in the presence of a vast and mysterious majesty. But most of all it is to be in the midst of a love so great it can enfold the world. Receive us as we rest our souls in thee.

O righteous Father, we confess that we have fallen short of that glory which thou hast intended for us. Often our striving has been against one another instead of for thee. Often we have drowned out thy still, small voice, or, hearing it, refused to listen. Accept our confession of sin, and restore us to the company of thy people.

Lord, God of the nations, hear us as our hearts join the chorus of intercession this day for peace based on justice. Let there be born in this world an order of international harmony based on a universal conviction that all men are brothers in thee. May nothing we say or do stand in the way of that event, and may our lives count in the balance with those who bring it to pass.

O great God of the church, we pray for each other as we worship together. May the prayers offered in this place, both spoken and unspoken, be granted according to thy wise providence. May all barriers that separate and divide us be broken down, making us one body with Christ our Head. And as we go forth about the business of this week may those among whom we labor be aware that we have been with Jesus. We offer these prayers in his holy name. Amen.

1

Reformation Day

O *God,* whom we could not seek hadst thou not first sought us, we thank thee for the good gift of faith whereby mere men hold converse with thee. We thank thee for those times when our own faith has been strong and we have been sure that thou art indeed our Father. We thank thee more for the faith of others—the constant faith of the praying church, the faith of the saints made real in the movements of history—which buoys us up when our faith flags. We thank thee, Lord, for faith.

O Lord, who hast so made us that we despise chains, we thank thee for the good gift of freedom; for that freedom of the soul which grows in Protestantism, and for that freedom in our social life which is guarded by democracy. We remember with stern self-appraisal that no freedom is true liberty save only the liberty wherewith Christ hath made us free from sin and death. Make our love for righteousness strong and deep that we shall need no ruler save thee.

O Father, who out of thy love didst make man to love and to be loved, we thank thee for the good gift of fellowship; for fellowship with thee that judges and heals us, and for fellowship with one another whereby life is made joyful. Let the loneliness of our hearts be ended by the knowledge that thou art with us, and may the hours spent with thee make us worthy of the love and companionship of other men.

Almighty God, who by the grace of faith hast given us to live in freedom and fellowship in this thy good and beautiful world, and who dost desire that thy will may be done in the world as it is in heaven, grant us to hear the call whereby thou dost summon the church to be thy people, and to go forth from this holy place to make all places holy, by the power and in the name of Jesus Christ our Lord. Amen.

2
Reformation Day

O *Lord, God of hosts,* we praise thy name that thou hast chosen to make thyself known to us in the radiant lives of men and women. Glorious and beautiful is thy creation in all its parts, yet the roar of an avalanche is not so grand as the voice of a prophet, nor is the petal of a rose so beautiful as the soul of a Christian mother. Give us seeing eyes to behold thee in the lives that touch us whether great or small.

O thou who dost speak to those whose hearts are attuned to hear, we thank thee for those men in whose consciences thou didst plant the seeds of the Reformation. We praise thee for our heritage and our mission as Protestants, a universal priesthood called to the service of Christ. Grant us in this generation a great thankfulness, and a great desire to fulfill our calling by being in this place truly a people of God setting forth in word and deed the gospel thou hast entrusted to us.

O thou tender Shepherd, great Father God, who dost love thy children more than we can love ourselves, receive our prayers for ourselves and for one another. Forgive us our faults, and give us power to overcome them. Take away our fears and our loneliness by being thyself our mighty fortress and our great Companion. And teach us how to save our lives by losing them in loving concern for others, near and far.

And grant, O Lord, that our worship this day may turn our lives outward, that the vision of thy goodness to us may chasten our proud wills and uplift our downcast hearts, so that our prayers and our deeds from this day forward may be directed wholly into the struggle of good against evil, of truth against falsehood, according to the example and by the power of our Master, Jesus Christ. Amen.

1
Reformation Sunday

A lmighty God, our Father, who by thy son Jesus Christ didst reach out to us hands of love, we are met this day to reach out to thee hands of faith that our hands and thine may be clasped together. Help us in these moments to know verily that we are thy people and thou art our God. Impart to us such light upon the dark problems of our lives that we may be able in all things to be brought into closer touch with thy victorious power. Bury all past errors and failures in thy forgiveness as we frankly confess them to thee, and make all future days better by the blessed grace of obedience.

On this Reformation Sunday we thank thee for the great heroes of Protestantism, who broke the shackles of fear and churchly dictatorship from the human spirit and taught us once more the great lesson of St. Paul, that each of us is brought to God by his own faith and his own humble prayers. We bless thy name that our forefathers won for themselves and for us the right to worship according to the dictates of conscience and not according to the dictates of church and state. Make us worthy of this great privilege, that freedom to worship may not be an occasion to neglect the things of the spirit but an occasion for each of us to come to thee with greater faithfulness, and that freedom in this nation and the world may have as its support a loyal and godly people worthy to be free.

Hear us, O Lord, as we pray for all free churches in the world that they may be true to their heritage; for all authoritarian churches that they may be true to the Christ who is the Head of all churches; for all leaders of men and all nations seeking peace that they may be brought face to face with the God of peace in whose service alone true peace and freedom are to be found; through Jesus Christ our Lord. Amen.

2
Reformation Sunday

O God, our heavenly Father, we praise thee that we, each one of us, can come to thee at any time in prayer. We know how many doors in this world are closed to us; how mayors and governors and presidents and kings are hard to see; how sometimes even our friends are so busy that they have no time for us when we are lonely or perplexed. But thou, the most high God, art ever more ready to listen than we are to pray. Help us in this hour of worship to be still and know that thou art God, and that thou dost care for us.

For many of us, O Lord, the path to thee is cluttered with weeds because we have not used it enough. Grant that by use this day the path may be cleared, so that we will find it easy and natural to seek thee on other days. Here in thy church we are one with each other and with thee. May the oneness and strength we feel here go with us to our homes and places of toil, making our hours of labor more fruitful, our hours of rest more peaceful, and our hours of leisure more purposeful.

On this Reformation Sunday we remember with thanks that we are heirs of the great Protestant tradition of the priesthood of all believers. We thank thee for the religious freedom that is our birthright. But save us, Lord, from neglecting the responsibility that is part of that freedom. Since the open Bible is our right and privilege, let the holy book not be closed to us. Since the Christian way of salvation is ours to walk in liberty, let us not by neglect find ourselves instead on the selfish way of perdition. By the prayers we offer this day, by the ministry of thy holy church, by the great and holy memories of those who have gone before, by every good influence of faith and hope and love, seize us and make us thy people; by the mighty mediation of Jesus Christ our Lord through whom we pray. Amen.

1

Canvass Sunday

O *thou eternal God,* our Father, we keep our tryst with thee this day as is our custom, to acknowledge that we are thy creatures who aspire to become thy children. All week long we are reminded that we are part of the material universe. All the voices of the world, the radio, the television, the press, and our own lesser desires, proclaim it. Getting and spending we have spent our time, and, alas, wasted much of it. So we come to thee on thy Holy Day to be reminded that we are not only creatures of sense but children of the Spirit as well, made to live and move and have our being in thee. In the mood of worship we would attune our hearts to hear thy voice of gentle stillness. In the silence of adoration we would make keener our spiritual senses that we may better know and have joy in what is beautiful and what is good and what is holy. Calm the turbulent waters of our troubled minds with the peace which passeth understanding.

As men in every nation under heaven turn their thoughts to thee this day, grant, we beseech thee, that the act of worship forge the chain of brotherhood. Bind all those who call upon thee in a fellowship stronger than hate can break, that shall free mankind from fear and establish the heart of thy kingdom.

Having taught us what it is to be thy children, brethren of Christ, go back with us to the world of material things that we may see that that, too, is part of thy kingdom. Help us to get honorably and to spend wisely, and to share the gifts of thy bounty generously. Kindle our hearts with the flame of love that glows on thine altar, that as we go out into the world of men this light may glow in the market place as well; through Jesus Christ our Lord. Amen.

2

Canvass Sunday

O *thou whose blazing glory we behold in the light of the sun,* whose serene beauty smiles upon the placid face of the moon, whose mighty power sends some stars hurtling through space and holds others spinning in their fixed orbits through the centuries, thou faithful and righteous God, we thank thee that thou hast given us voices to praise thee, hearts to love thee, and minds to know thee. Receive our prayers of adoration!

O Lord, God of the church, we offer special prayers today for our church as we make together in these next few days our pledges of money for her support throughout the coming year. We pray for these men and women, our friends who will visit in our homes on thy behalf. Consecrate them, we beseech thee, for this holy ministry amongst us. Cleanse us all of any enviousness or stinginess or pettiness of spirit. Let nothing rob us of the great joy of giving, that as we offer our treasure to thy church it may be a visible sign of a deeper offering of ourselves to thee.

O heavenly Father, in this month when church people in this land of abundance are giving tangible proof of their devotion may an increase in vitality be felt in every part of the church throughout the world. May our prayers follow our gifts to missionary stations at home and abroad, and may the sacrament of sharing bring forth new courage and hope in those who strive under the sign of the holy cross for the causes of thy kingdom.

O God, we pray that in this hour of worship thy Holy Spirit may invade our lives and make us thine. Having praised thee with our voices and adored thee in our hearts, may we go forth to serve thee with our hands and glorify thee in our whole lives, for the sake of Jesus Christ thy Son. Amen.

Thanksgiving Day

O thou Giver of every good and perfect gift, we are moved to pour out our gratitude for the good things of life. For the pulsing rhythm of living: the beating of our hearts, nighttime and dawn, springtime and harvest, sunlight and rain, hunger and fullness, seeking and finding, all within the tender care of thy providence, we bow in grateful praise.

Our contrition on this day, O generous Father, is for the meanest sin of all, the sin of ingratitude. So profound is our selfishness that the denial of our least desire or personal ambition can blot out of our vision the infinite bounty of thy daily gifts. We are shamed as we recall the Hebrews in the wilderness shouting for joy as they thanked thee for the perishable manna, the martyrs singing praises in the arena, the pioneers of our land going forth in the springtime to plough their rocky fields with prayers of thanks for survival and for love. Forgive us, we beseech thee, and to all thy gifts add yet one more, the gift of gratitude.

God of the nations, thou hast blessed our land with prosperity, and power, and liberty. May our prosperity be an occasion for generosity; our power, an occasion for responsibility; and our liberty, an occasion for self-discipline in holy exercises and good works. Open our ears to the warning that all good gifts turn to ashes when they are hoarded. Let our blessings bless the world by the grace that is in us.

O loving Lord, who gavest us the unspeakable gift in the outpoured life of thy Son Jesus Christ, grant us in thy mercy so to receive this gift that our lives may be kindled by an answering love great enough to purify us completely. So may we be, in our homes and in our world, part of thy redeeming work. Having prayed in Jesus' name, may we live to his glory. Amen.

1

Forefathers' Day

O *thou God of our fathers,* we thank thee this day for the heritage thou hast entrusted to us. We did not make ourselves. It was thou who gavest us the gift of life. We did not select the place of our birth. It was of thy mercy that we were born in this land of plenty and of promise. Nothing have we done to deserve the blessings of freedom. They are ours by inheritance, having been given to our ancestors by thee and defended by them through the years at great cost. Save us, O Lord, from the prodigal errors of foolish pride. May this treasure we receive be safe in our hands. Humbly we bow in thanks to thee.

Humbly we ask yet one more gift, the gift of good stewardship. Since we have freedom to worship, let us worship in spirit and in truth. Since we have freedom to think, let us neglect not the discipline of the mind, but face clearly and without prejudice the issues of life. Since we have freedom of speech, give us courage to speak the truth even when falsehood is popular. Since through no virtue of our own we live in a land where there is freedom from want, let our hearts be compassionate toward those who through no fault of their own live in lands where pestilence and starvation are rife. Since thou hast called us to live in this tremendous age and hast endowed us as a people with both wealth and power, save us from the awful fate of those who have broken their trust with thee. As we have inherited freedom from our forebears, grant that we may also inherit from them stern qualities of honor and high hopes of thy kingdom. Receive this church and her people, and use us to thy glory, through Jesus Christ our Lord. Amen.

2

Forefathers' Day

*A*lmighty *God,* who hast been the dwelling place of men in all generations, age after age the faithful have sought thee and have found that of thy faithfulness there is no end. We remember with thanks the heritage we have from our spiritual forebears: their faith whereby they set out to found a spiritual kingdom on these shores, their devotion whereby they endured untold hardship, their vision whereby they discovered the ways of freedom. Forgive us our little faith, our feeble devotion, our cloudy vision. Since all their strength was thy strength, do thou renew our zeal in our holy religion that this day may find their children stout and eager to go forward in a great tradition.

O Father God, who dost love us all as if each were the only one in the world, give us grace to pray for one another. We acknowledge that we often worship as if our own great need were all there is when about us are those with burdens greater than ours: burdens of loneliness and grief, of fear and doubt, of pain and loss, of pride and self-pity, of confusion and misunderstanding. Grant us a measure of thy holy love that we may sincerely pray for one another, and praying in faithful love instead of petulant desire find to our surprise that our own burdens have disappeared.

When the hour of worship is over, send us forth, O God, a people mindful of the company we have kept. As we fight our battles and undertake our labors remind us daily that we belong to the Pilgrims, the Reformers, and the saints of old, and to our fellow Christians in China and Hungary and Alabama today. May this awareness save us from trivial ambitions and set our hearts on the goals of thy kingdom; for we pray in the name of Jesus Christ thy Son. Amen.

3
Forefathers' Day

O *thou Great Soul of the universe,* infinite God, thou who didst lead Abraham from Ur to Canaan, who didst guide Israel from the Red Sea to the Promised Land, who didst set the face of Jesus like flint to go to Jerusalem and didst constrain our forefathers to cross the wide seas, we meet this day to praise thee for the hardy pilgrims of all ages and to seek thy present help in our own pilgrimage.

O God of all the nations, we thank thee for our native land. Remind us of the heritage of freedom and piety, which we did not win, but which we received from those who bought it with their life's blood. Inspire us to fulfill the yet unattained dream of a nation where there shall be liberty and justice for all. But save us from idolatrous nationalism. Let no flag ever stand between us and the cross of Christ. May we be a people under the discipline of God, obedient to thy will alone.

O Father God, we thank thee for the blessed and holy discontent which comes upon us as we contemplate the excellence of Christ and those others in history who have been completely his. We thank thee for that vision of ourselves as thou dost will us to be: strong, pure, generous, and brave. Keep that vision ever before us and increase its magnetic power that by thy holy compassion we may be drawn in worship from what we are to what we ought to be.

O God of all that has been and all that is to be, receive our broken lives and make them whole, and having healed us, use us for the healing of others, that our words and our deeds and our prayers may be the manifestation of thy Holy Spirit in human history. Hear this, and all our prayers, both spoken and unspoken, for we pray in his name whom thou didst send to make us one with thee. Amen.

Universal Bible Sunday

O *God,* whose ways are higher than our ways as the heavens are high above the earth, we join the company of those in all places and in all ages who have bowed before thee in worship. We are the ignorant in search of wisdom, the guilty in search of forgiveness, the mortal in search of life eternal. Hear, O Lord!

O thou All-Wise, we offer thee special thanks this day for the Bible, the holy book wherein thy word is revealed, like fresh, cool water, like vibrant life within the good earth in springtime, like music in a violin fashioned in love by a master craftsman. Open to us the Scriptures, we pray, as thou didst to men of old, that we, too, may receive thy holy word.

Open our eyes to behold wonderful things out of thy law; quicken our consciences that we may know our need of thy forgiveness; comfort our souls with the assurance of thy continual pity; and help us to find in thee the satisfaction of our hearts' desire. Give us grace to study whatsoever hath been written of thee by holy men of old, with reverence and trust. Feed us upon the bread of life; give us to drink of the water of life freely.

Grant us grace, almighty God, to be true keepers of Christmas. Give us eyes to behold the heightened expectancy of little children, the softening of hard and crusty hearts, the light in the midst of darkness, the hope that outlasts despair. Let not the garish and feverish and blatant abuses of these days deceive us, for we would be among that faithful fraternity of shepherds and kings and humble souls of all the years who in giving their lives to thee have been enabled to receive the gift of thy life to them in Jesus, the Son of Man, thy holy Messiah, in whose name we pray. Amen.

Advent Communion

O *God, our Father,* who didst come into the world in a new and living way with the birth of Jesus our Lord, be with us anew as we stand on the threshold of another Advent season. Help us as we seek to prepare our lives for his coming. If we are to entertain him as our holy guest, our lamps must be lit and our doors open to receive him. Remove from our lives all obstacles: all cherished sins that make us uncomfortable in his presence, all beloved falsehood and self-deceit that cloud our vision. So shall the expectant joy of the shepherds be ours, and so shall this Christmastide again be holy with the songs of angels.

We begin the celebration of our Lord's coming by observing the celebration of his death. Grant that the significance of the sacrament may not be lost upon us, for we know that even over the joyous day of Jesus' birth there hangs the shadow of Good Friday. Teach us that in our lives as well as his life Christmas and Good Friday and Easter are all part of the same plan, and that the plan is good. Comfort with this knowledge all for whom the Christmas season is one of dread instead of joy. Let the prayers of this church go out to all who suffer in mind, body, or spirit. May the holy balm of friendship heal broken hearts and remove stubborn fears. May the simple faith of the Holy Child lift up all that are cast down.

Look upon thy wayward world with compassion, O God. Strengthen all those who labor for peace among men. Reassure those who falter and doubt, with a new outpouring of thy blessed love. May the light of Bethlehem's star shine again as a symbol of the invincible hope of man for peace among men of goodwill. We pray in Jesus' name. Amen.

O *Father God,* come to us again as we stand at the gateway of another Christmas season. As silently and by night thou didst steal into our world so long ago in the form of a human babe, so, we pray, while we sit here in silence do thou steal into our lives in the Spirit of that same Christ. As the dark night was made light by the light of a star and the cold stable was made warm by the warmth of thy holy presence; so lighten our dark lives and melt our cold hearts, we beseech thee, by coming in unto us to share with us the days in which we live.

We come unto thee bringing our burdens with us: our sins, and griefs, and hatreds, and fears. But here before thine altar all burdens fall from our backs like ice from a mountain under the spring sun's rays. Here our minds are made sensitive to a light our eyes cannot see and we know that this is thy world, and that we are thy people, and that insofar as we live in thee thou makest us to dwell in safety. With the ancient psalmist we sing, "The Lord is my light and my salvation, whom shall I fear? The Lord is the strength of my life, of whom shall I be afraid?"

We praise thee that our sins are forgiven, our fears removed; why then, should we bear ill will toward any man? As the autumn rains cause living water to bubble up once more through dry springs, washing them clean and filling them with clear, pure water; so does thy Spirit fill our hearts with faith and hope and love, washing away all the poisonous thoughts that made us languish in confusion. Grant that we, being healed, may use the strength thou givest us for the healing of others, and that the fellowship we have in thy church may be a haven of refuge, a tower of strength, a storehouse of power for us and for all thy children everywhere; through Jesus Christ our Lord. Amen.

*G*racious *God,* come and abide with us for a while as we stand upon the threshold of the Christmas season. Not even the black clouds of conflict can quite blot out the light of the Star of Bethlehem, nor can the blast of bombs still the song of the angels. Grant us in this time of testing, eyes that can see, and ears that can hear the voices of eternity as well as the voices of earth.

We stand under conviction, O God, when we remember thy judgment. We have not loved thee with all our heart and soul; we have not loved thee with all our mind and strength; we have loved ourselves first and our neighbor afterward, and, sometimes, thee not at all. Arouse us by thy judgment and grant us the blessed gift of repentance that we may turn about from ways of death to ways of life, to thy glory and our salvation.

We thank thee, Lord, for the world-wide observance of the Advent season. As people of all nations prepare for the annual celebration of the coming of the Christchild may it be a bond of common devotion among us. While we decorate Christmas trees by German custom, rejoice in the traditions of Holland's St. Nicholas, and sing the carols of England and France and Russia, may we be stirred to prayers and labors of peace. And may the Christchild's faith roll back the fog of fear from all peoples that we may discover the truth that we are one family and thou our Father.

Be present with thy church, O God, in every place where her members find themselves; in pulpit and in pew, in home and market place, let the church be the church, the living heart and hands of Christ believing and preaching, praying and doing the deeds of thy kingdom. Hear us, for we pray in the name of him who is our Head, Jesus thy Son. Amen.

O *thou living God,* we bow in reverence, at the beginning of another Advent season, before the holy mystery of life. How marvelous is the life hidden behind a baby's questing eyes, a baby who can grow up to be a criminal or a saint. In this darkest of the seasons of the year we prepare to celebrate the birth of a baby who grew up to be Immanuel, "God with us." For this with wonder we give thee thanks.

O God, who hast so made us for thyself that we cannot be at rest until we find ourselves in thee, let the great discontent of our souls be satisfied by a new and more certain belief that thou art indeed our Father. As Jesus came into the world to be the fiery Judge of evil and the shining Savior of good, so may he enter our lives to condemn and purge all in us that is unpleasing to him, and to restore thy lost image within us. As Jesus was born to be thy Son, so may we be born again to be thy children.

O heavenly Father, as the Prince of light and love descends once more to a world of darkness and hate, let him be met by such a fervent welcome of prayer in his church throughout the world that even his mighty power may be magnified. May the approach of Christmas pour quenching torrents upon the rising fires of hostility in men's hearts, and may the universal human hunger for peace be matched by an equal desire for justice.

O Lord of life, as thou didst send John the Baptist to prepare the way for the coming of thy Son, send us from this place to be the messengers of his Advent wherever we shall be. May the presence found about the holy table be carried into homes and offices and shops as we give evidence in our lives that we have been with Jesus. Hear this and all our other prayers both spoken and unspoken, for his sake. Amen.

O *thou ever-living, ever-loving God,* our Father, we worship thee this day for thy glory and thy mercy. We adore thee for thy mighty acts of creation: for the majestic rhythm of the seasons, each with its own beauty and its own discipline; for the incredible wisdom thou hast displayed in the fashioning of our bodies, so that without our giving it a thought food is transformed into bone and muscle and nerve, and night by night we turn to thee in slumber, confident that when morning comes thou wilt return our bodies to us refreshed by the miracle of sleep. For these and all thy blessings we thank thee.

We glorify thy name for thy greatest deed, wrought in Christ Jesus, who, by his humble coming, his gracious ministry, his dreadful death, and his glorious resurrection, has given us faith to believe that thou dost love us. We praise thee that here in this house, as we give free rein to those unspoken but life-giving reassurances of thy Spirit within us, we receive abiding convictions that even on dark days will enable us to know that life is good, that with thy help no obstacle is insurmountable, no defeat disastrous, no hour utterly hopeless.

Lead us forth from this place today as those who know where they go and why. Make the blessed purposes of thy kingdom our purposes. Use us, mind and body and soul, for the waging of thy holy war against the powers of spiritual wickedness, in our own lives first, and then in the world wherever evil is found. As John bore witness in the wilderness to the coming of our Lord, so may we be messengers before thy face crying out in word and deed for the true repentance by which thy people may be saved, through the same Jesus Christ, our Lord. Amen.

A *lmighty God,* who hast so ordered thy universe that each ebb
tide is followed by its flood and each black night by its
bright dawn, we thank thee for the regular return of the day of
worship and of the Christmastide. Bind us together once more
in the communion of prayer, and lift us again into thy holy
presence.

O Lord, we thank thee for these days when we are deeply
aware of our kinship to other people. Hear our prayers for mail-
men and all postal workers laboring in frenzied but orderly
confusion to deliver our messages and gifts; for people with cold
feet who stand on sidewalks with bells in their hands asking for
money with which to bring cheer to cheerless places; for policemen unsnarling our traffic jams with patient efficiency; for
harried salespeople and all others for whom these days are full
of shrill demands; and for those in hospitals and elsewhere who
feel left out and forgotten. For these and all whom thou lovest
we offer prayers of intercessory compassion.

O God, we pray for the unity of the broken Church of Christ.
As we meditate upon the wonder of his holy advent, and as we
contemplate the fruits of his coming in all the centuries, may it
bring us nearer to one another. Grant us wisdom to separate the
essential from the nonessential in our disagreements with our
fellow Christians, and the humility to learn as well as to proclaim. Let our divisions shrink into their proper size as our
common faith increases.

O Lord Jesus Christ, thou Light of the world, overcome our
fatal affection for darkness by turning our desires from the goals
of evil selfishness to those of holy love. So may the dawn of thy
splendid radiance be, not a terrible judgment to be dreaded, but
a glorious vindication to be welcomed with wondering delight.
We pray in thy name. Amen.

6

O *almighty God,* our Father, we worship thee this day with prayers of thanksgiving and praise. Of all the creatures thou hast made we are of thee most blest. To man alone thou hast given the priceless gift of the knowledge of good and evil whereby, if he will, he may become thy child. To man alone hast thou given the privilege of worship whereby he may know the joy of fellowship with thee. To man thou didst come that first Christmastide to abide with him in Jesus as a Man among men. We praise thee, we bless thee, we adore thee for that glory as of the only begotten of the Father which we ourselves may behold if we belong to him. For the gift of life which thou hast lent us we give thee thanks and praise.

Since thou hast given us so much, O Lord, and we have returned so little, we must offer every day prayers of confession and of penitence. Considering the great privileges we have of knowing thee and being members of thy kingdom, we have produced little to justify thy favor. Too many of our high ideals have been expressed in words only. We have tried to do half-heartedly what needed our whole heart, soul, mind, and strength. Grant us the grace of thy forgiveness, O Lord; transform our lives by the indwelling of thy Holy Spirit; and enable us to give ourselves, heart and soul, to thee.

And now, having praised thee, thanked thee, confessed unto thee, and made our peace, we turn our prayers outward and remember before thee the needs of others. We pray for all the homes to which this church ministers that they may be full of thy love and dedicated to thy glory. We pray for the world in which we live that the seeds of thy kingdom may burst into bloom in our day by the power of Christ, the Lord, in whose name we pray. Amen.

*O*ur *Father,* we thank thee for thy patience with us. Week after week we come confessing that thou art God, and that we owe unto thee allegiance. But week after week, we go out and live lives that are not such as should be lived by thy children. Instead of facing our deficiencies we find unholy comfort in criticizing the foibles of one another. Forgive us, O Lord, our frequent sins, our easygoing ignorance and neglect.

O God, of thy faithfulness and patience there is no end. At this we marvel and bow in penitence. We offer thee this day not only our songs and prayers, but also our lives. Grant us the courage to mean business in life. Give us the faith and the wisdom to tie our hands and hearts and heads together and all to thee. Let our words of devotion become our bond. Let our good intentions crystallize into deeds.

As the advancing winter sends forth his icy cold, we thank thee for the blessings of warm homes and for the goodness of wool blankets and snug overcoats. But even as we thank thee we are reminded that there are many, both in our land and throughout the world, for whom these things are unknown luxuries. Our Father, touch the hearts of us who have with compassion for those who have not, that of our Christian love and not of their envious hatred may come a juster distribution of this world's comforts.

And lead us all, we pray thee, to a higher knowledge of thee. Grant that in this service of worship our hearts and minds may be lifted into thy presence, there to receive light and love and joy. We pray in his name who was born in a stable yet liveth and reigneth with thee in glory everlasting, even Christ Jesus thy Son. Amen.

8

A*lmighty Father,* Lord God of hosts, we praise thee this day
for thy mighty acts: for the creation of the world full of
beauty and wealth; for the creation of all living things, especially
mankind with eternity in his heart; and above all for the mighty
Christ-deed whereby a way is opened unto us from the wilderness of despair to the heavenly city of hope. As we contemplate
the deeds of mercy thou has wrought both in the world and in
the lives of men, teach us likewise how to go about doing good
for thy sake. Take the good intentions that bud so profusely in
our minds and water them with thy spirit of powerful love that
they may not die a-borning but blossom into acts of body, mind,
and spirit, deeds that shall heal broken hearts and bodies, deeds
that shall bring stature to our souls and honor to thy kingdom.

Hear us, met together in thy name, as we pray for thy grace
on behalf of the needy, the sick, the lonely, and for those who
know not how to pray for themselves. Be to all thy children as
thou art unto us, the friend of the friendless, and the never-
failing hope of the hopeless.

Descend, we pray thee, in these moments of worship and make
them glow with the warmth of thy living presence. Help us to
be still and know that thou art God, yea, that thou art our God,
that we may climb on stairs of faith to high places of devotion
and of peace.

And send us forth when our worship is done with lives more
wholly dedicated, souls shriven of sin, hearts laden with mercy
and minds with wisdom, to labor and to strive that the gates of
thy kingdom may be opened unto all thy people; through Jesus
Christ our Lord. Amen.

O *thou eternal God* whose name has long been praised in this house, and throughout the world since the dawn of man's life upon this planet, draw near once more, we beseech thee, and receive our worship. Guide us in our praise that we may keep unbroken the chain of adoration that binds the centuries together.

O Lord, who hast bound us together in thy holy church, we thank thee for the blessed privilege of belonging to each other and to thee. We thank thee for our fellow Christians here and everywhere, for those whose songs and petitions are strange to us. Let thy Holy Spirit dwell wherever men gather in the name of Jesus, overcoming by the unity of Christian love all barriers of race, nation, or language. So may thy church draw peoples together that nations may be led in ways of peace.

O thou faithful Shepherd of all mankind, we pray for this congregation. Some of us are full of joy in celebration of Christmas; may our joy be pure and compassionate and contagious, touching all among whom we walk with the blessings of these days. Some of us are afraid and lonely and weary; O our Father, may our communion in this place renew our flagging faith and restore our heart for the battle yet another week. Surprise us all with thy clear call to Christian discipleship in the still, small voice that speaks in answer to our prayers.

And having kept thy tryst with us in these our prayers do thou send us out to do thy will, out into the Christmas world all spangled with the beautiful and the monstrous tokens of men's varied concepts of how the season should be kept. Send us, O Lord, with a firm purpose in our hearts to be like John of old who prepared a way for the coming of thy Christ into the hearts of men. In Jesus' name we pray. Amen.

1

Nativity Sunday

L *ord of all the days of our years,* we thank thee especially for the marvelous day when we celebrate the birth of Christ. Among our most precious memories are those other Christmases we have known: those of our childhood, full of the delight of new possessions and the joy of giving some trinket whose value was only the love of which it was the symbol; joyful Christmases when the whole family was gathered about the hearth from far-away places; Christmases when joy was mixed with the pain of recent sorrow, and dark ones when the shadow of tragedy hovered near. Yes, even for the dark Christmases we thank thee, for always the light of the star has meant to us a hope in the midst of despair.

Grant, O Lord, that Christmas this year may be best of all, not because the gifts are most lavish and the dinner most sumptuous, but because we have caught a clearer glimpse of that light of faith and hope first lit by Jesus, the light 2,000 years of shining have not been able to dim. Give us, O God, both the humility of the shepherds and the wisdom of the Magi that we may be among those to whom is given the privilege of the heavenly visitation. And grant us grace to offer the Christchild the gift of a humble and contrite heart.

As the light of the Holy Star shines down once more upon children living in caves and holes, may the hearts of those who have much be moved by the sufferings of those who have little. May the same holy compassion that led thee to send thy beloved Son to save us, move us to deeds of brotherhood, that no child may be cold or hungry this day or any other because thy church was unfaithful. Hear us, for we pray in his name at whose coming the angels sang, "Glory to God in the highest, and on earth peace among men of goodwill." Amen.

2
Nativity Sunday

W e *praise thee, O God;* we acknowledge thee to be the Lord. All the earth doth worship thee, the Father everlasting. To thee all angels cry aloud; the heavens and all the powers therein. To thee cherubim and seraphim continually do cry, Holy, Holy, Holy, Lord God of hosts. Heaven and earth are full of the majesty of thy glory. We praise thee, O God; we acknowledge thee to be the Lord.

We thank thee, Father, for the wonder of Christmastide, for the renewal and deepening of old friendships, for the messages from afar that reopen beloved and forgotten memories, for the shared joys of childhood, and for the pleasure of giving. Above all, we thank thee for thine unspeakable gift, for in Bethlehem's Child thou thyself didst come to us.

We confess with shame, O God, that though thy light has shone in our midst 2,000 years, we have seen it only once in a while because we have been so much in love with our darkness. Grant, we pray thee, that in this hour of the world's need we may cast off all our precious sins. Give us the expectancy and the willingness of the shepherds that we may go straightway to the Bethlehem of our souls and that the promise of the ages, the promise of thy peace, may be fulfilled for us this day.

Let all who sing of the blessed coming of Christ, wherever they are, be ready to receive his spirit into our lives. Be born once more, O God, in humble hearts. Release upon us the mighty power of thy love. Stem the tide of proud hate, and hurl back dark ignorance. As the light of another Christmas Day dawns let the people of God arise clean and brave and obedient to thee, ready for thy labors; for we pray in his name who was a child and a man and thy Son. Amen.

Christmas Day

O *God, our tender Shepherd,* we thank thee that thou hast brought us to this day. Truly the promise of the angel is fulfilled who said, "I bring you good news of a great joy which shall come to all the people." The glory of thy wondrous gift is upon a million hearths. Even in homes darkened by pain and grief the blessed Child is present today with the holy gift of hope. The whole earth sings for joy, and it is all thy doing. We thank thee, O God, for Christmas.

Our Father, we thank thee for the wonder of childhood, for the ecstasies of delight in little things. We thank thee for every pleasure of friendship and family love. We thank thee for thy steadying hand that has guided us through dark valleys and over rough, steep ways. We thank thee for all the joys of life and love and labor made greater by these days.

We offer special prayers for all whose sorrow is greater because it has come in this time of joy. We remember before thee the people of nations at war who live in dread, those who have been visited by calamity or disaster in the midst of celebration, and all who live in darkness of their own or others' making. Let not the clouds of man obliterate the stars of God, but let the Light of the world enlighten every darkened soul.

And, Lord, let not the floodgates of compassion be stopped tomorrow just because it is Christmas no longer. We bless thee that the Lord Jesus Christ who was born on Christmas Day is still here, and will be with those who seek him as before. Make it hard for us to go back to our old ungenerous and unforgiving ways. Because Christ has been born to us again let all our days be Christmases and all our hours beautiful with the songs of angels; through the same Jesus Christ our Lord. Amen.

Christmas Carol Service

*L*ord *of all being,* throned afar,
   Thy glory flames from sun and star;
Center and soul of every sphere,
Yet to each loving heart how near!

Sun of our life, thy quickening ray
Sheds on our path the glow of day;
Star of our hope, thy softened light
Cheers the long watches of the night.

Grant us thy truth to make us free,
And kindling hearts that burn for thee,
Till all thy living altars claim
One holy light, one heavenly flame.

Our Father, we thank thee for the lofty lines of hymns by which our hearts are lifted up to thee as if on wings. We bless thy name for the treasure of faith and hope and love that lies within the covers of the hymnal. Guard us lest we sing half-heartedly or thoughtlessly. Unlock for us the faith of the ages, that as we sing thy praises our spirits may be healed of sin and doubt. Particularly in this season as we sing the ancient carols of Christmastide, may our lives be made glad with those tidings of great joy which shall be to all people. Make us a singing church whose lives bear witness to the sacred beauty and harmony of thy gospel.

And may the songs of thy church throughout the world be thy voice speaking to all those whose lives have not yet bowed down to Christ. Let this season be one in which thy blessed evangel is heard as at no other. So shall Bethlehem's Babe come again to the world's people and the peace he heralded draw nearer. Hear us, for we pray in his name. Amen.

Sunday After Christmas

O thou in whose sight a thousand ages are but an evening gone, thou who from everlasting to everlasting art God, Ancient of Days, Lord of all the years, abide with us this hour as we pause upon the threshold of the door which soon will close forever on the old year. As we stand between the years grant us, we beseech thee, a glimpse of eternity.

O heavenly Father, we have praised thy name for Christmas. Today, we thank thee for all the days after Christmas. Take the deep feelings of this Christmastide and keep them for us to use in all our tomorrows. Let our joys and loves be stored up like rose petals in a jar to be brought out and enjoyed again on some day not so glad. And if these days have brought us hurt and sorrow, let even these minister in us to sympathy and compassion for others in thy world more bruised than we. O God of the holy Christmas days, be thou our God through all the year.

O God of peace, the cries of war are not yet stilled. The year is all but gone, but its works of goodness and justice and love are barely begun. The sons of men have been so busy with their own folly that there has been little time for holy tasks. As the sun sets on this year's last day may we be filled with dread enough to fear the bloody fruits of sin, and with love enough to undertake the blessed works of righteousness.

Go with us through the gate to the new year. Enable us to be thy partners in determining the shape of things to come. Let thy Holy Spirit within us renew us day by day. Awaken the vision of thy glorious kingdom of love that every year may be indeed *anno Domini,* the year of our Lord. We pray in his name. Amen.

Last Sunday in the Year

L ord, thou hast been our dwelling place in all generations. Before the mountains were brought forth, or ever thou hadst formed the earth and the world, even from everlasting to everlasting thou art God. For a thousand years in thy sight are but as yesterday when it is past, and as a watch in the night. On the threshold of another year we pause and acknowledge that this like all others is thy time and we are thy people.

We thank thee for the gift of a new year. We confess that we did not do well with the old one. Many days in it we are ashamed of, when we think that they are inscribed forever in thy book of life. We would give much to erase the hasty word spoken in anger, the thoughtless deed done in selfishness. Help us, O God, to fill the days of the coming year so full of service and of love that all past failures may be forgotten.

O Father, tenderly we remember before thee all who have passed through the portals of death during the year that is past, especially those near to us, whose passing has left an emptiness within us. We thank thee for thy precious promises by which we have faith that they are safe with thee. Fill our loneliness with the hope of eternal life and consecrate all holy memories unto increased devotion of our lives to thee and to thy kingdom.

Lord God of hosts, dwell mightily in thy world these coming months. So strengthen the counsels of sanity that war may come no more. As men in their extremity turn to thee let true penitence prevail. May the fear of thy judgment bear fruit not only in wisdom, but also in compassion, that the sufferings of the world's people may be abated. Let the power of faith and the light of freedom dwell in us, for we put our trust in thee. We pray in the name of him who is the same yesterday, today, and forever, even Christ Jesus our only Savior. Amen.

1

Epiphany Sunday

O great and terrible God, thy ways are higher than our ways as the heavens are high above the earth. The power and beauty and magnificence of thy universe cause us to say with the psalmist, "What is man that thou art mindful of him, and the son of man that thou visitest him?" The poor words of prayer that come to our lips seem inadequate to express the great and deep need of our souls. Yet thou hast taught us in the holy Scriptures that we ought to pray and not to faint. Thy Son Jesus Christ has told us that mighty and holy as thou art, thou art still our Father. Prayer turns to praise upon our lips as we contemplate how great a thing it is that we can hold fellowship with thee. We praise thee for prayer as we pray.

We recall with wonder the story how long years ago wise men brought presents of gold and frankincense and myrrh to a babe in Bethlehem. We have little gold and nothing as precious as frankincense and myrrh to offer thee, but such as we have we lay upon thine altar this day. We give thee our lives, blighted by sorrow, twisted by sin and error, that thou mayest renew them and remake them into that image of thee in which they were created. We give thee the fellowship of this thy church, that this house may be thy house and the hearts of these people thy dwelling place in the world. We offer thee our spirits, weak, afraid, broken, to be healed and strengthened by faith in thee for the victory of righteousness. And we thank thee that in all the world no gift is more acceptable to thee than the humble and contrite heart of a child of thine.

Send us upon thine errands in the place where we live. Thy kingdom come. Thy will be done in earth as it is in heaven, beginning with us. We pray in the name of Jesus, our Savior. Amen.

2

Epiphany Sunday

O *God, the Father Everlasting,* as the needle of a compass whirls and waves until it finds its true course in pointing north; so we in our lives wander and stray until we find our true purpose in thy will. Complete thy creation, O Lord, we pray thee, by making us wholly thine.

O living Christ, to whom wise men from the East brought precious gifts, we, too, come to thee today with gifts. We give thee the gold of wealth that thou mayest perform a miracle. Transform our dollars into faith and hope and love for thy needy ones. We give thee the frankincense of worship. Take our prayers and transform us by them, making us clean and strong instead of impure and weak. We give thee the myrrh of suffering. Take whatever sufferings and privations we are called upon to bear and use them like the sufferings of thine own holy cross unto the salvation of the world.

O Holy Spirit of the living God, who choosest the hearts of men for thy dwelling place, come into our hearts and abide with us. Speak to us the word that we need: courage in time of fear, faith in time of doubt, warning in time of temptation, forgiveness in time of sin, all-conquering love in time of hatred, undying hope in time of despair; and let thy words abide with us until they have wrought in us thy holy will.

O triune God, Creator, Savior, Counselor, make thy presence felt and feared and heeded in all places where people live and die. Inspire thy church with a new wisdom and power equal to the greatness of this hour. And send us forth, each one of us, to our several tasks, battles, and ordeals with the courage and confidence that belong to the people of God. Hear these and all our prayers, we beseech thee, for the sake of Jesus Christ thy Son our Lord. Amen.

1

O eternal Christ, we would offer before thee acceptable sacrifices to thy glory and our salvation. We have all come to the end of a year of our lives, and we lay that on thine altar. A poor gift it is, full of selfish hours, blundering blind errors, sins of omission and commission. But there are in it good days also, times when a lesson was taught by thee and learned by us, times when with true penitence we found thy forgiveness, hours of our time that we truly saved by using them in love for the goals of thy kingdom. Accept these hours given to us as our gift returned to thee.

O Lord, we are taught in Holy Writ that dedicated lives are a good and acceptable sacrifice unto God. We here dedicate ourselves to thy service in this coming year. Take these lives of ours and set them on the right path. Help us to discover the real purposes for which we were born into the world, and to be true to those purposes. Save us from the horrible error of wasting the precious hours and days in futile wanderings after false gods and spurious goods. Let this year to come be set before thee as a holy offering that thy saving love may find in us, not an obstacle, but a channel through which it may bless thy people everywhere.

Above all, help us to know that all years are years of our Lord and of his Christ, that our times are in thy hands and underneath are the everlasting arms of God. In quietness and confidence we offer our lives as gifts to thee. Lead us, Lord. Lead us in thy righteousness, for it is thou only who makest us to dwell in safety. We pray in the name of him who is our Savior and our Lord, even Jesus the Christ. Amen.

O *God,* before whose face the centuries rise and pass away, age after age the children of men have called upon thee in prayer and in each generation have found that of thy faithfulness there is no end. From everlasting to everlasting thou art God. Glory be to thee, the Father Everlasting!

O God, who art the Author of all things good, we thank thee for the priceless gift of the Christchild whom thou didst give to men upon the first Christmas so long ago. Wise men on camels and afoot, by ship and by railroad and through the sky on metal wings, have converged upon his cradle in every century to do him homage and offer him their best gifts. We have come here today in the noisy chariots of the twentieth century to join the worshiping throng. Empower us to offer him the only gift worthy of his notice, our heart's whole devotion.

O Lord of the centuries, as we stand today between the unchangeable past of which we are not proud and the unwon future of which we are afraid, we are deeply aware of our great need of thy help. Overcome our foolish pride by making us witnesses of thy majesty. Overcome our weakness by enfolding us in thy power. Overcome our self-centeredness by giving us a vision of thy kingdom, with affections wide enough to match that vision. So may our prayers turn outward and our hopes for the future be expressed in the prayer we were taught by the Master: "Thy kingdom come, thy will be done."

O God, who didst send us the Lord Jesus Christ to be our King, let no idol with feet of clay keep us from total allegiance to him. Yea, by his grace we dare to pray that thy church may become a company of kings, a royal priesthood, the people of God, through the power of Jesus Christ our Lord. Amen.

O God of all the universe, we adore thee for thy great majesty revealed in towering mountains, in broad plains, in mighty oceans, and in the changing skies above us. Yet we know even greater awe when we behold the wondrous stature of Jesus Christ and the soaring souls who, led and empowered by him, have followed in his train. We praise thee, God, for the grandeur of men and women in tune with thy Holy Spirit.

O God, hear our special prayers of intercession for thy church in all the world. We thank thee for the steadfast love which thou hast shown toward those who are thy people in the midst of pagan civilizations. Continue that grace without which the church cannot be the church. Chasten its pride, reform its errors, bind up its disunity, eradicate its fears and doubts. Grant that each minister and layman, each missionary, each woman and child in the church, may be in his family and his community and among his people a true witness to thy gospel.

O great Source of all life, we bless thee for thy provision for our every need of body and spirit, for the fruits of the good earth, for wealth of forest and mine, for beauty and knowledge and virtue. We thank thee for our fellow men who serve us: for farmers and builders, for physicians and policemen, for laborers and engineers, for teachers and executives, and for all who work in the halls of government and commerce. For all these who do their duty in faithfulness we thank thee.

Our Father, having heard the prayers we offer together do thou hear also the unspoken prayers of our hearts. Attend our confession of sin, our plea of weakness, our fears and doubts, our ambitions and our aspirations. Use our prayers, we beseech thee, to restore in us thy lost image, through Jesus Christ our Lord. Amen.

O living God, who art the same yesterday, today, and forever, whose power is from everlasting to everlasting, and whose goodness never faileth, we, from the midst of our little day on this melting planet, presume to lift our hearts to thee in worship. We acknowledge with sorrow the poverty of the gifts we have to offer thee. Whatever good there is in us we owe to thee our Maker. Only the evil can we call our own, for that we have chosen of our own free will. But such as our lives are we offer them to thee, O God. For thy sake we would give up the cherished hatred and covetousness. We acknowledge that vengeance is thine and we pray for the spirit of forgiveness, for only in forgiveness can we share that image in which we were created, even thine own image.

In this month when our eyes are turned toward the future with alternate hope and dread, we pray that our part of that future may not be such as will give us further shame. We believe in thee, O God of mercy and justice; help thou our unbelief. Help us through our worship to build the ramparts of faith against the enemies of doubt and fear. Train us ever to look to our Captain, Christ, for light and strength in times of need. And use us to thy glory.

We remember in love before thee, our Father, all those to whom the door to the future is grim and dark and without promise: the hungry and the destitute, the lonely and the distraught, the sick and dying and those who love them, all those who know not the consolation of a firm faith in thee through Christ; descend upon them by thy Spirit, we pray, and show them that Christ is the open door to thy kingdom, a door no man may shut. Hear us, O God, for we pray in his name. Amen.

*A*lmighty *God,* King of the universe, how presumptuous we are to offer praises to thee! Thou art so great; we are so small. Thou art so free; we are so dependent on thee that every moment of our lives is thine to give or to withhold. Yet there is that within us that must praise and magnify thy holy name. Great and marvelous are thy works. Glory be to thee, O Lord Most High.

O thou All-Merciful, God the Father, we who live in comfort in the midst of winter offer prayers of intercession for all who suffer cold and hardship in these days: for all servants of thine who minister in primitive lands where danger and difficulty are part of every day, for those whose homes have been destroyed and whose means of livelihood taken away, for the sick who have no medicine, the cold who have no shelter, the hungry who have no food, and for all the lonely and friendless. And may deeds and gifts follow our prayers.

O God, who hast given us gifts without number and beyond measure, grant us these gifts more: to be grateful and penitent. Let us not be content with a faith that makes us satisfied with ourselves as we are, but rather cause us to long for the better life of those who follow hard after Christ. Quicken within us the hunger and thirst after righteousness.

Before we part this day we offer thee our prayers for one another. May those who have come in fear return to their homes in faith. May those who have come with selfish schemes depart with holy resolves. May those who have come with hearts and eyes downcast set out with hearts and eyes uplifted; and may all of us together go forth as good servants of thine to do thy will with confident gladness because our lives are stayed on thee; through Jesus Christ our Lord. Amen.

O God, our Father in heaven, age after age the faithful of all generations have sought thee and thou hast not turned them away. From the depths of war and famine and pestilence, from beds of pain, grassy lawns beside open graves, and every day in happy homes the world around, the prayers of humanity ascend unto thee and thou dost hear and heed. Wrinkled, tense foreheads become relaxed and smooth again. Frowns of anxiety turn to smiles of peace. Furtive eyes are first downcast in shame and then uplifted in hope once more in the presence of thy Holy Spirit. We thank thee for thine eternal faithfulness as once more we seek thee in prayer.

Receive our petitions this day for all thy children everywhere. We remember before thee the President of the United States, the Governor of this Commonwealth, and all others elected by the people to serve in our government. Confound all their selfish designs and lead them to wisdom and humility great enough for their great tasks. We remember in thy presence the sick, the bereaved, and all those in pain, that all may know thy nearness and receive thine ever-present help. And we pray for all those who are forgotten by others, those whose names we cannot call but whom thou knowest, the aged and the lonely and those who know not the way of salvation, that thou mayest find for them the way from darkness into light.

In this service of worship we offer our own lives unto thee. Weak we are and soiled with many a shoddy thought and deed. But we have heard the voice of Christ who tells us that even the wayward are dear in thy sight. Drive out all our fears and sins by thy grace, make us over into that divine image we have marred, and use us today and always in the work of thy kingdom, through Jesus Christ our Lord. Amen.

O *our Father*, since thou hast taught us that we should love our neighbors as ourselves and since, in this shrunken world all men are neighbors, hear these our neighborly prayers. We remember before thee today thy children who are hurt in body or in spirit. There are those who lie on beds of pain for whom the hours pass like years with dragging feet. We pray for them, O God, that they may be renewed by the courage and hope of faith. There are those who are unemployed, who are forced to watch the family resources dwindle while there seems to be no chance for work. Whisper to them again the promise that unto those who seek first thy kingdom thou wilt add all other things needful, and inspire the members of thy church to lend a helping hand where it is needed. There are those in faraway lands wrecked by the ravages of war who have felt the pangs of hunger every day for many years, watching their children grow up thin and misshapen. Keep alive their hope by the promises of our great free nation, and give us Americans the strength of character to turn our promises into deeds.

O God, we remember also those in our community and in our state and all over thy world whose spirits are stunted and puny because they have never been taught the lessons of thy holy gospel. Renew within us the missionary zeal of the apostles. Let the light of thy truth shine so brightly in thy church that those outside may see the difference it makes and long to glorify thee with their lives.

And as we have prayed for our neighbors here and everywhere, so now we pray for ourselves. Help us, O God, so to believe in thee that we shall lose our lives in Christ. For so alone shall we find them in thy kingdom. Hear us, for we pray in Jesus' holy name. Amen.

6

O God, *our heavenly Father,* our hearts are uplifted in thy presence to receive the kindling touch of thy Holy Spirit. Like the light of the moon upon the water, like the sound of voices singing in harmony, like the warmth of the open fire to frosty hands, like the hearty greeting of a good and trusted friend, so is thy worship unto us, O Lord. To pray is to rejoice in the never-failing nearness of thy life to us. As moment by moment we take the good, sweet air into our lungs to give life to our bodies; so in prayer we receive thee into our hearts to give life to our souls.

In these moments we are drawn close to one another. We cannot contemplate thy great love for us and at the same time harbor resentments against our fellows. No matter how greatly we have been wronged our injury cannot approach the debt of folly which thou hast forgiven us, and since thou hast forgiven us we are moved to forgive one another.

May our prayers together work to the increase of love within us. Being purged of jealousy and hate and anger, let our lives be made strong in the labors of thy kingdom. Let thy church be a winning, outreaching church to which thy children shall be attracted and in which they shall find thy peace.

We offer here our petitions and desires. Make our country holy as well as great, that she may not fail in her hour of testing. Heal the spiritual blindness of those who know not thy peace, that the eyes of their souls may be opened to the light of thy countenance. Lift from us all the burdens we bring here that we may go forth from this place with joy to bear the burdens of others. Hear us, for we pray in Jesus' holy name. Amen.

*D*ear *Lord and Father of mankind,* we approach thy throne together this day to lay our common needs upon thy heart. We come from many homes and from many differing stations, but our needs are much alike. We need renewed confidence that life is good, that it is worth living, that the high ideals and aspirations handed down to us by our forefathers are not shadows but hard realities. We need guidance as we seek to find those paths wherein we should walk if we would be worthy of thy calling. We need vision to see opportunities for service and to avoid the ways whereby we do injury to the feelings of others. We need faith and hope and love to give us power to overcome obstacles, endure pain, and face uncertainty. And we come to thee who knowest our needs before we speak and who art ever more ready to hearken to us than we are to pray to thee.

We pray for each other as we wait in thy presence. Let no one whose heart is open to thee go empty away. We pray for the homes of this parish where there is sorrow, where there is sickness, where there is anxiety, where there is insecurity. Let the love thou givest us in Christ go out to those who need it most to help each one in his condition.

And we pray for the community of which we are a part, the city, the state, the nation, the United Nations. So let the church be *thy* church that thy freedom-making truth may be heard and heeded in the councils of those who lead us. Let thy Spirit so invade the hearts of men that the powerful may be endowed with the higher graces of true greatness, that the stratagems of peace may outstrip the stratagems of war and thy will be done upon the earth; through Jesus Christ our Lord. Amen.

O thou omnipotent God, we bow in thy presence to acknowledge thy terrible glory. All things belong to thee for thou didst make them. It is thou who sendest the storm and the biting cold. It is thou who settest the bounds of our lives in this world so that they begin and end. It is thou who ordainest the eternal laws of right and wrong; so that in obedience we find life and joy, and in disobedience we find frustration and death. Too long we have lived without recognizing thy power. Too long we have ignored the mandates of thy holy will. Take our lives offered to thee in worship. Make clear to us how great a thing it is to trifle with the most high God. Reset our sights so that they point to the true goods of love and life and not to the fool's gold of passing pleasures. Awaken us to the stern realities of life so that our daily choices may be made aright.

And having made our peace with thee, having set our houses in order, do thou hear us as we pray for others. We pray for the Governor of this Commonwealth and the President of the United States and all others in high positions of authority. Teach them, we pray thee, that to lead is to serve, and give them wisdom and compassion to know and to meet the real needs of the people.

We pray for thy church throughout the world as the hearts of her members are opened to thee in worship. Though we are of many nations and races, teach us that our oneness in thee is greater than our variety of tongues and colors. Let us know thee as Judge, that by repentance we may come to know thee as Father. So may thy light shine in us to the salvation of all thine erring children. We pray in Jesus' name. Amen.

O *thou who art our Father and our God,* we bless thee that of thy faithfulness there is no end. Age after age the sons of men have sought thee, and age after age thou hast hearkened to their prayers. We thank thee that thy mercy and thy righteousness endure forever. We are thy people. Thou hast made us. Be thou our God!

We have not enough thanked thee, our Father, for thy daily gifts. Sometimes with blasphemous hearts we even take credit unto ourselves for things thou hast given us; today we acknowledge that it is thou who hast made us and not we ourselves. All that we have thou hast given us: health of body and mind, skill of head or hand, the privilege of being citizens of a land where bread is given us daily, friends and dear ones to love and by whom to be loved; for all thy gifts we give thee humble and hearty thanks.

O Lord, let our prayers go out through thee to those who stand in particular need of thy love. We pray for all in our parish who are sick or who bear the burdens of anxiety or sorrow. Be thou the great rock in the desert whose cool shadow gives respite from the merciless sun. And be thou very near to all thy children for whom nobody else will pray or who know not how to pray for themselves.

Father, we would offer thee our whole selves this day. Weak are we all and dying. How halfhearted is our devotion! But thou canst take our weakness and thereby magnify thy power. We have dared enter thy very presence; do not let us get away from thee ever again but seize us and make us building stones of thy kingdom. Hear us, Father, for we pray in the blessed name of thy Son our Lord. Amen.

O *Lord, our Lord,* how excellent is thy name in all the earth. Out of weakness thou hast made strength. When we consider thy heavens, the moon and the stars that thou hast ordained, what is man that thou art mindful of him, or the son of man that thou visitest him? Yet thou has crowned him with glory and honor. Thou hast put all things under his feet. Thou madest him to have dominion over the work of thy hands. O Lord, our Lord, how excellent is thy name in all the earth.

Heavenly Father, how marvelous is thy creature, man. How wonderful is his body. How full of divine possibilities is his soul. Yet how miserably short of thy holy purpose for him has he fallen. Thou didst place us in this world to make of it a paradise, and instead we have made of it a hell. Receive our confession of penitence, O gracious God, and renew us by thy forgiveness that we may become indeed children of thine.

O God of mercy, draw near and comfort all those who have come to this place with burdens of doubt or fear or guilt upon their hearts. Let this be indeed thy house. Let the might of thy Spirit be round about us to comfort and uphold. May none go away without being lifted up and empowered by thee.

O great Leader who didst send thy Son Jesus Christ, to show us the way out of the darkness of time into the light of eternity, give unto us the gift of obedience. Where we cannot see the way ahead help us to follow him in confidence that he doth know the way. And in moments of uncertainty let his voice call and his hand beckon lest we stray or fall. Let our lives here dedicated be made fit for service in thy kingdom beginning today. Hear us, for we pray in Jesus' holy name. Amen.

O eternal God, we thank thee for that in man which responds to thy Spirit's call. As long as man has lived on this planet a holy restlessness has turned the eyes of his soul outward and upward in hungry search after things eternal. We rejoice as we recall how wonderfully the upreaching aspirations of man and the downreaching of thy love are met and blended in Jesus, giving our prayers a straight road to thee.

Save us, our Father, from deafness of the spirit. Let not our prayers be so voluble and clamorous as to drown out thy word to us. Give us grace, daily, to be still and know that thou art God, receiving from thee guidance when we are confused, strength and courage and hope when we are downcast, and in all times of temptation the constraint of thy righteous Spirit.

O loving and tender God, who, since thou hast made us, rememberest that we are dust, be close, we pray thee, to all thy children who are afraid this day. Let all who find that of their own strength they cannot uphold themselves or their loved ones, discover the comfortable power of the everlasting arms. Let not fear be a barrier between thee and thy children, but may it turn them back from ways of death to ways of life abundant.

O Lord God of hosts, who makest the wrath of man to praise thee, and who canst bring strength out of weakness, we offer ourselves to thee in the eternal struggle of the powers of good against the powers of evil. We are powerless by ourselves. But we long by thy might to cast all evil and hate out of our lives and out of the world. Go with us, we pray thee, and be our God for we would be thy people. Empower us through Christ Jesus thy Son, our Lord. Amen.

O *thou almighty God,* who didst watch as men raised the pyramids out of the desert sands, who didst see the mighty sequoia trees when they were little shoots breaking through the crust of the earth into the light of day, we gather in thy house today to sing thy praise and to acknowledge that even from everlasting to everlasting thou art God.

We are met here, O Most High, at the call of One who lived a life like ours yet by his words and mighty acts persuades us to believe that we may look up into thy face and call thee Father, yea, even that we may find through him a kinship to thee, that we may share with him the inheritance of everlasting life. O thou living God, who hast kept this faith alive in thy holy church down through the centuries, do not forsake us now, but kindle anew in us that brightest and best of all the hopes of man.

Being persuaded that we, like Christ, are meant to live with thee, may we discover by thy grace a kind of life worthy of thy company. Grant us a holy scorn for all meanness and baseness and pettiness that we behold within us. May we see in ourselves and in every human being in the world not only that which is, but also that which thou dost mean us to be, that in our families, our communities, our nations, and our societies of nations we may live as children of God.

O heavenly Father, who hast imparted to us the great good news of thy limitless love for men, may it not find us halfhearted heralds, but may we become inspired like the saints of old to proclaim thy gospel both in the words we speak and in the lives we live. So move those among whom we live to rejoice with us in the faith whereby we may be freed from sin and death; through Jesus Christ our Lord. Amen.

13

O thou who art the Author of liberty, we bless thee this day for the restless hunger for freedom thou hast planted within the human spirit. Bring confusion to all demagogues and keep the fires of liberty bright and hot. And as thou dost keep us ever vigilant against those who would steal our political and economic freedom, keep us likewise on the alert against those who would forge chains for our spirits.

Deliver us, O holy God, from the hypnotism of the flesh that binds us by desire for sensate pleasure. Make us masters and not servants of our bodies. Drive from our minds all selfish pride and wanton prejudice. And break the fetters of greed and covetousness that bind us, that we may stand before thee as free men and women to declare our adoration and receive power to glorify thee in deeds of love. Build within our souls a room for the Heavenly Visitor, thy Holy Spirit, who shall warn us when we are about to sin, restrain us from error, guide us in doing the right, and empower us to endure hardship and resist temptation.

Make vivid before us in this service of worship the Christ whom we follow. Help us to make his life a part of our lives, his experience of prayer and service, of death and life, a part of our experience, until we become in a measure like unto him, that by us and by thy holy church in all the world, the sons of men may know that thou hast sent him. Hear us, O God, for we pray in his name. Amen.

14

O God, Father of our Lord Jesus Christ and our Father, Creator and Sustainer of all that is, Source of all that is good, Author of all that is holy, we come to thee as our custom is to be with thee in the intimacy of worship. We bring contrite confession of all the many errors of our lives; thou dost bring forgiveness and wisdom to free and to guide us. We bring thankfulness for all the good gifts thou hast poured out upon us; thou bringest more gifts and hast in store treasures more marvelous than our little minds can imagine. We bring the problems of life, weighty and small, that hinder us in the race of life; thou dost bring relief in faith and hope, and power and purpose to speed us on our way refreshed. We bring lives that are empty or base or crass, but thou art here with thy transforming Spirit to enter our lives and convert them into the likeness of the Master, if we will only give thee entrance. Let in thy cleansing light, and fill us with thy love that we may begin this day the endless sojourn with thee that is heaven.

Our Father, as thou dost teach us the eternal importance of our own lives may we be given a new sense of the importance of all human life. In a day when lives are cheap and many are selling lives to get dollars for themselves, infuse into thy church the spirit that caused Jesus to teach us that even the least is infinitely precious to the heavenly Father, and make us tremble at the wrath of One who said it is better never to be born than to cause one of thy little ones to stumble.

As we receive thy love in worship make us not only receivers but also transmitters, that thy love may be multiplied in us for those whom we may serve; through Jesus Christ our Lord. Amen.

A*lmighty God,* we call thee King and Creator, Savior and Redeemer, Lord of hosts, Judge of nations, Soul of the universe, and so thou art, but thou art so much more than these and our tongues are so clumsy. Yet something there is within us that bids us cry unto thee in psalms of adoration. O thou who rememberest our frame and knowest that we are dust, we thank thee that we are such dust as is able to rise up and praise its Maker. Receive our homage, we pray.

O God, who art concerned for thy people and who dost not depart from the faithful, we pray for all who strive for righteousness in the midst of great difficulties: for men in public life who endure censure because of high principles, for all who have chosen to live amidst hardship and loneliness for the sake of thy kingdom, for those who struggle in causes which though losing are righteous—grant to all these the vision of Elisha that they may see the fiery horses and chariots of God and know their strife is not in vain.

O thou omnipresent God, may our fellowship in this hour be rich with the heightened awareness that thou art in us and about us as closely as the air we breathe. Let thy life touch our lives in very truth as a flame touches the wick of a candle. We come to thee full of darkness. Grant us not only light for ourselves but also the power to shed light for those around us. O Lord, make us eager to be thy people.

O Lord, who didst create man that he might be thy comrade, suffer us not to miss this our holy birthright. Let not our love for things thou hast created be a substitute for our love for thee, the Creator. May we be in this world as those whose eyes are opened to the glory of the eternal world in which thy Son doth reign as King. We pray in his name. Amen.

O Lord, our God, we thank thee that thou hast given us to live in a time like this. Terrible it is with possibilities for evil, and uncertain for those with eyes that see only the present. But by thy grace thou hast given us to know the holy purposes of thy creation, how thou didst create the world to have loving fellowship with thy children. Thousands there are in all nations who know that all men must be brethren or die. Millions of people, moved by compassion, have given gifts to save the lives of other millions around the world. Thou hast given us the tools of radio and aviation whereby the words and workers of the gospel can be taken to every outpost of thy kingdom. Be with us as we strive to make thy church a beacon of divine hope and power and joy in the midst of human despair.

We pray for all our fellow Christians far and near: for all those behind the iron curtain who are demonstrating by simple steadfastness the triumphant heroism of the saints; for all those here in our own nation and our own community who face personal trouble with a serene spirit because they know that no matter what may come thou art still their Father. Give us all, O God, a portion of the wisdom and the radiance of Christ, wisdom by which to understand the follies and hopes of our own hearts, radiance by which to share that wisdom with others.

We pray for one another and for our fellowship in this church. Help us to worship in spirit and in truth. Direct our minds into thoughts of our sins and the good traits of others lest in judging we may be judged. And take this service of worship as an open door into our lives whereby thou mayest come in and dwell with us mightily, healing our ills, forgiving our sins, strengthening our wills, and increasing our devotion to Jesus Christ, through whom we make our prayer. Amen.

17

E^{ternal} *God,* we bow our hearts unto thee in worship with grateful amazement that thou dost desire the prayers of men. Thou hast given us all we have, food and shelter, work to do, others to love who love us, even life itself. And we can bring thee nothing that is not already thine own. Even so there is a voice within us that bids us pray, for thou art listening, and so, returning the love whereby thou didst create us, we offer thee our prayers.

O thou great Deliverer, who hast spared us the anguish of guilt from great and conspicuous sins, save us, we beseech thee, from the little sins that can destroy us just the same. Save us from pettiness, from the hard and unforgiving heart, from lack of gratitude, from foolish pride that seeks a reward for doing only its bounden duty, from censoriousness and conceit; lest the door whereby thy Holy Spirit would enter our hearts should be blocked. Sweep us clean that we may be fit temples for thee.

Holy Father, hear our prayers offered in this place for all thy people. Especially do we pray today for those whose names we do not know, but whose lives like ours are full of joy and pain, of love and fear, of goodness and evil. We pray for the people who are afraid of us because they do not know us, and for all in countries far and near whom thou knowest as thy children. Let our prayers be a bond between us that shall grow until it is stronger than the forces that thrust us apart and all thy people shall be one.

O God, who hast blessed our coming in, and hast made our assembly beautiful and holy with thy nearness, do thou likewise bless our going out. May thy gospel be with us wherever we go, that we may walk among our fellow men as those who walk with God; through Jesus Christ thy Son our Lord. Amen.

1

Boy Scout Sunday

E *ternal God,* we bow our heads and our hearts in thy presence. We remember that thou hast made us. We recall that thou didst send us thy Son, Jesus Christ, to die that we might live. We remember that nothing good is ours save as thou hast given it to us. For all good gifts of life itself we return our thanks to thee, O Lord.

Our Father, we remember with shame how shabbily we have used thy holy gifts. Thou hast given us hearts with which to love, but instead we have used them to envy and boast. Thou hast given us minds with which to think, but instead we have allowed ourselves to be influenced this way and that by demagogues and ax grinders. Thou hast given us hands with which to serve, but instead we have used them to satisfy our greed. Grant, O Lord, that in this service of worship we may be restored to the path in which thou madest us to walk. Fill our hearts with thy love, our minds with thy truth, and our hands with thy work to do.

We thank thee this day for boys, little and big, particularly for Scouts and Cubs and Explorers. Grant that the high ideals of honesty and obedience and kindness and cleanliness and reverence that they so easily recite, may be not only imprinted on their minds but also incorporated into the habits of their daily lives. Grant to their leaders wisdom that they shall inspire them to become men worthy to be called God's children. And help all of us who belong to the older generation so to live that the society we bequeath to our children may cause them to rise up and call us blessed, full of justice and freedom and lovingkindness. We pray in Jesus' name. Amen.

2

Boy Scout Sunday

O living, loving God, the brightness of whose glory the centuries cannot dim, we praise thee that thy greatness is to be the guard and guide of those who have no other hope. To the fatherless thou art a Father. To the weak thou art a mighty defense. To those who plan and perpetrate evil thou art the thunder of judgment. And to all who seek the right way to life thou art the mightiest Friend.

We thank thee, O God, for all boys. We bless thee for their enthusiasm, their curiosity, their hunger after high adventure. Give unto them, we pray thee, a great and restless dissatisfaction with all save the noblest kind of manhood. We tremble when we contemplate the kind of world we have given them to live in, and pray that thou wilt give them a faith equal to the day.

We remember, our Father, that there are many who by neglect and sin have been denied the privileges of the good life: boys in this community whose lives have piled up on the rocks of crime and perversion; boys throughout this nation both in slums and in palaces whose spiritual growth is being stunted by parents who turn their backs on thee; boys left orphaned by war in nations around the world who grow up wild like animals in the jungle. Quicken the conscience of the world, O God, lest this treasure of youth be lost, and aid mightily all Christian efforts to seek and to save.

In this hour of the world's great need, let all who call themselves Christians turn back, we beseech thee, from the mad scramble after personal gain and pause to consider what ways may yet be found to avert the global disaster that hovers over us. As the pressures of hatred rise let there come from thy holy church a matching tide of good will and understanding; through Jesus Christ our Lord. Amen.

Race Relations Sunday

O Lord, in a world of things we sometimes come to believe that we are things, nothing more. Yet we are taught that by faith we can become no less than children of the living God. Multiply, we beseech thee, the signs of thy nearness. Join us to that stream of singing people who have lived out their steadfast lives in the conviction that thou art the Father of men.

Merciful God, we are ever conscious to our shame that what we preach we fail to practice and what we believe we fail to live. Grant us the forgiveness that brings forth greater faithfulness. We are so wrapped up in our own joys and sorrows, hopes and fears, that we become insensitive to the terrible needs of our fellow men and unaware of the visions and dreams of mankind for a better world. Grant us grace to forget ourselves in selfless labors, that the prayers of mankind for thy kingdom's coming may be answered.

We remember before thee, O Lord of mercy, all thy children who walk in peril to body and soul. Especially do we pray for those who live where racial tensions run high and impatient men would settle differences of opinion by violence and lawlessness. O God, let understanding and tolerance and patience born of faith in thee prevail. Let no stones or hot words be cast by any who have not first confessed their own sins. And guide us all lest we demand of others a level of righteousness we are not ready to apply to ourselves.

O God, having heard these our spoken prayers do thou hearken also to the silent petitions which each of us offers in the privacy of his own heart. Make us one body in our need and in our common loyalty to him who is our hope, thy Son Christ Jesus, in whose name we pray. Amen.

Brotherhood Sunday

G*reat and good God,* we rejoice in the holy privilege that in Christ we may look to thee and call thee Father. Open our minds to see that if we are to have thee for our Father, we must own all thine other children as our brethren. Brand upon our hearts the word of Christ that a man who loveth not his brother whom he hath seen cannot love thee whom he hath not seen. Thou hast made us to live together. Increase in us, we pray thee, the spirit of brotherly love which alone can make living together a joy and not a curse.

Righteous Father, begin with us. Draw us closer to thyself, that so we may come closer to each other. Level the walls of class and race and political faction, of social and economic station, until we have found the unity of our common humanity in our common allegiance to our common Lord. Strike at the divisions that separate us Christians one from another in denominations, so that thy church itself may be a witness to unity and not to schism. So increase the hunger of men for fellowship and understanding that they will not be satisfied until the world is at peace.

Teach us how to live with those whose opinions differ from ours in a spirit of mutual humility and respect, since we all stand in need of repentance. In all the modes of human togetherness —the family, the school, the church, the state, and the family of nations—let the pervasive power of holy love increase. So shall a miracle of discovery occur: in seeking the heart of a brother man to be his friend we shall find in his heart thy Spirit, and having fellowship with him the gates of heaven shall be opened and together we shall be in thy presence where there is fullness of joy and peace forever; through Jesus Christ our Lord. Amen.

1

Lincoln and Washington

O *blessed God,* in this month when our minds are refreshed by the memory of men of stature, we come to thee in thankfulness for thy merciful gift of great souls. We praise thy name that thou hast raised up in all times of great need men who have been equal to the times. We thank thee for George Washington, the father of our country, and for Abraham Lincoln, the savior of the Union. We bless thee for saints and geniuses of our generation, and of all generations. And above all others we thank thee for that One who is the source and criterion of all greatness, Jesus Christ our Lord, thy Son, our Advocate, in whose name we pray.

Almighty God, as we meditate today upon the quality of greatness may we have fellowship with those who have been master craftsmen in the workshop of life. Teach us, too, O God, the lessons of victorious living, that we, likewise, though in humbler ways, may do thy bidding and bring thy holy will to life in the affairs of humankind.

As we consider our world and its great needs, we pray that now as of old thou wilt send us leaders of greatness and of vision. Inspire the youth of our age with high thoughts and holy purposes. Grant that this church may have a part in the training of those who will wisely lead and those who will wisely follow. And dwell with us mightily that ours may be a heavenly fellowship, both powerful and good; through Jesus Christ our Lord. Amen.

2

Lincoln and Washington

O *Lord,* thy majesty calls forth our praise as thy love doth awaken answering love in our hearts. Thy universe stretches out about us vaster than our imagination. Yet thou didst create the universe. Thy splendor surrounds us on every side, bearing witness to the infinite power whereby thou dost rule all things. With reverent awe we make our prayers of adoration.

O God of all great souls, we give thee special thanks for Abraham Lincoln and George Washington whose natal days we celebrate this month. Grant, we beseech thee, that in the tremendous day in which thou hast given us to live there shall arise leaders of like stature to guide the nations aright. May the youth of this generation be inspired to seek for themselves those qualities of noble self-discipline and generous self-giving which are the marks of true greatness.

O righteous Father, as we worship thee beholding our lives in the light of thy holiness and remembering our debt to all by whom we have the blessings of freedom, knowledge, and true religion, fill us with a proper discontent with ourselves as we are. Let us be satisfied with no ideals save the highest, with no quality of life save that which comes from pure and steadfast obedience to thy calling. And having given us the vision of faithful discipleship do thou grant us the power to become indeed children of the Most High.

O Lord of love, we have covenanted together to pray for one another and care for one another. Round about us in this holy place are heavy hearts, and wills sorely tempted, and lives grown weary beneath heavy burdens. May our prayers for one another bring us strength beyond our own, and may we go forth better able to fulfill the tasks to which thy providence hath assigned us; through Jesus Christ our Lord. Amen.

Great Birthdays

O God, our Creator, who dost hold in thy hands the beginning and the end of history, we thank thee that into every age thou hast sent men of greatness to lead thy people out of bondage. We thank thee for the mighty men of our own nation, for George Washington and Thomas Jefferson and Abraham Lincoln and all the rest, who founded and preserved these United States as a bulwark again political tyranny for the peoples of the world. We thank thee for Louis Pasteur and Thomas Edison, for Darwin and Reed and Carver and other men of science, who have unlocked the mysteries of the material universe in which we live. We thank thee most of all for those giants of the spirit who by their intuition and their devotion to thee have opened the Book of Life and taught us the truth that makes men free: for Moses and the prophets, for Buddha and Confucius, for Francis and Luther, for Schweitzer and Gandhi, and above all others for Jesus, thy Son.

O God, we pray for our country which we love. Since in thy providence thou hast called her to a position of leadership, pour out upon this people a measure of thy Spirit equal to this hour. May greatness appear not only in high places but also on the street and in office and shop, in home and polling place, that this nation glorious thus far may not fail in her moment of destiny.

Grant in thy mercy that the cry of our great need in this generation may not be unanswered. Choose from among our youth and call them to greatness in leading thy people from darkness into light. And inspire us in thy church with such an awareness of our mission that our petty personal problems may be swallowed up in a great outpouring of faith and hope and love that shall conquer the world, not for America, but for humanity and for thee. We pray in Jesus' name. Amen.

1

One Great Hour of Sharing

L ord, save us from the curse of being flippant and frivolous with holy things. As we worship may we remember Moses who took off his shoes lest he defile the holy ground where thou didst visit him. May we be like the prophet Elijah who wrapped his face in his cloak lest he behold thy glory and die. So may we come into thy presence with a wondrous sense of how great a thing it is to worship the living God. Nothing have we done to earn the great gift of living in thee. Our feeble good intentions condemn us by their poverty and pettiness. Yet thou didst create us in thine image and didst send thy Son to direct our hearts toward thee.

Heal us, body and soul, as we wait in thy presence. As a cool hand to a troubled forehead so may thy Spirit be to our spirits, O God. Take all our hatred and envy and pride and drown them in the forgiving love that pours from thy holy cross. Touch tenderly the seeds of faith and hope and love which thou hast planted in our souls, bringing them to life that they may grow. Plant firm within us the consciousness that we are thy children. So shall our fears be scattered and our confidence restored.

We remember this day all the thousands of churches in this land who participate in the One Great Hour of Sharing. May we give with open hearts unto our brother's needs, not for hope of glory, but out of the sense of kinship that comes when we recognize that all God's children are one family. Grant that this hour of sharing may bear fruit, not only in the relief of the hungry and the cold and the hopeless whom our dollars shall rescue, but also in the souls of those who give that they may grow a little more toward thy likeness who gavest all for us. We pray in Jesus' holy name. Amen.

2

One Great Hour of Sharing

O *thou who art from everlasting to everlasting,* who art the Alpha and Omega, the beginning and the end, there is no limit to thy care for men either in time or in space. We search the records of our race back to the dawn of life and find thee there planting the seeds of thy kingdom. We gaze far into the misty future, and as far as we can see thou art there shaping our destiny into thy perfect pattern. O thou great All in All, we rest our lives in thee.

O Father of all mankind, we thank thee especially this day for the ties of sympathy that bind all men together. We cannot behold the suffering of a fellow human being without in some measure feeling his pain. In the little world of this latter day make us good neighbors after the pattern of the Good Samaritan. Let none of us pass by on the other side, but let every disciple of Jesus Christ open his heart and his purse to help those less fortunate than he. May a generous compassion wash away the hatred and bitterness of the world.

O Lord, our God, who hast taught us by thy Son that whosoever would save his life shall lose it, but that whosoever loseth his life for thy sake shall find it, help us to find the solutions to our own lives' problems in service to others. We are weak and sinful; in forgiving the sins of others against us may we find thy forgiveness of our failures. We are proud and foolish; in beholding the heroism of those who struggle on against terrific odds may we be made humble and wise. We are selfish and ungrateful; may the joy of giving of ourselves in time and talent and treasure bring forth in us a true appreciation of our great debt to thee. We are afraid and lonely; may we find in helping one another the healing, empowering companionship of God; through Jesus Christ our Lord. Amen.

79

Lenten Communion

O *Father,* all our days should be so full of thee that there would be no need of special days in which to give thee thanks or sing thy praise or seek thy forgiveness. Yet because of our frailty we stand in constant need of prompting. We have forgotten thee and have wandered far from thy ways. Do thou remember our weakness, O Lord, for we are dust, and take the days of this lenten season which lies before us and consecrate them to the renewing of our souls.

As we meditate upon the terrible and mysterious events that culminated in the passion and death of Jesus, our Lord, let the warmth and beauty of his personality stir our lives as it stirred those other disciples of long ago. Teach us again that Peter and Andrew and James and John were humble men like us, full of doubt and sin, but when they met Jesus they became apostles with the stuff of martyrs in their souls. Give us, likewise, we pray thee, such a vision of the Christ that our lives may take on some of that radiance, that the fellowship of which we are a part in home and in church may glow with the warmth of heaven because thou dost share in it.

As we partake this day of the sacrament of our Lord's death, may the remembrance of his holy sacrifice both condemn us and lift us up. May it condemn all selfish pride, all thoughts of covetousness, all grudges harbored against a neighbor, all in us that is unworthy of the broken heart of God's Son. But also, may it lift us up with the knowledge that thou didst so love us as to purpose our salvation even at so great a cost. As thou dost continually offer thyself to us in Christ, so in this service do we offer ourselves to thee. Take the burdens from our backs. Free our feet from the sticky clay of selfishness. Lead us forth confidently as bearers of glad tidings to all thy people who wait for a word of hope. We pray in his name who is the hope of the world. Amen.

E *ver-living God,* We thank thee for the many ways thou hast made for us to know thee. The Children of Israel felt thy splendor when they beheld a mighty mountain uplifted to the sky. Others have been touched with awe by the wonder of life beneath a microscope or the flaming grandeur of the sky at eventide. Some have known thy holiness by the stirrings of nobility and faith in the spirit of thy creature, man. Open the avenues of prayer unto us, O Lord, that in this hour of worship we may know that thou art God.

We remember, our Father, as we enter the doorway of the lenten season with eyes open to the blackness of Christ's passion and the whiteness of his resurrection, that we are part of a company of millions in every land and of every race who share the despair of earth and the hope of the gospel. Let the observance of these holy days be rich and deep and alive. May the wonder of our common faith in Christ overshadow all our differences. Let the church be thy church united, strong, and true to her mission of peace.

O Lord of love and tenderness, draw near, we pray thee, to all thy children who are in trouble. Let those whose strength is spent find in this place a strength beyond themselves. Let our prayers carry our love through thee to all the homes of this parish where pain and fear and loneliness dwell. And grant that all those who have been forgotten of men may be assured that they are remembered of thee.

O God, recall us, we pray thee, to the main business of our lives. Long enough we have wandered in search of that which is neither bread nor true gold. Send us from thy house into thy world to be in it thy strong ambassadors. And in thine own way and time let thy kingdom come. We pray in the name and by the power of him whose life is given for the life of the world, even Jesus, our Lord. Amen.

Teach us, our Father, how great and terrible a thing it is to worship the living God. Bow down our spirits as we wait before thee, the Holy One. Grant us reverent hearts and expectant minds that our worship may be in spirit and in truth.

O Lord, King of creation, Judge of the earth, we confess that we stand under the condemnation of thy law. Like the apostle Paul we have rejected the good that we would like to have done in favor of the evil we despised. The glorious life of Jesus stands as a judgment upon our feeble and unfulfilled good intentions. Grant us, we beseech thee, a grander vision of him in these lenten days, that we may truly seek and find thy forgiveness, and find in him the kind of life thou madest us to live.

Our Father, who dost love thy children with a perfect and infinite love, we pray for all our fellow men. Especially do we pray for those in all places who this day lift up their prayers to thee in the name of Jesus Christ. Hear their prayers and answer them according to thy wise mercy, granting to all who pray the assurance of thy fatherly goodness and concern for them. And since we offer our prayers in concert to one God, do thou seize us by our prayers and make us one family, at peace with one another and with thee.

O living God whose dwelling place is the humble and contrite heart, we open to thee our hearts, bowed down and willing to receive thy spirit. Come in and abide with us, not only in this hour spent together in thy house, but as we go forth to labor and to serve in thy great world. As we go in and out among our friends and fellow workers may they notice in us a new spirit and observe that it belongs to Jesus Christ, in whose blessed name we pray. Amen.

Gracious God, we praise thee for this holy place. We thank thee for this hour of worship and all that it brings us of renewal and of strength. The bowed heads about us bear witness to our common need and our common faith. Nowhere in all our living are we so close to one another as when together we offer up our prayers and songs to thee. We thank thee for the goodly fellowship of which we are a part, and for the holy privilege of helping to bear one another's burdens.

Turn our thoughts in these moments toward Christ. Fill us with the knowledge of his life and death and resurrection. Inasmuch as we have failed to live up to his holy calling may our souls be stricken with sorrow. Inasmuch as we are here and now willing to turn from our evil ways to follow him may we be restored to his company and know once more the joy of his salvation. Inasmuch as we are weighed down by the fears and pains and griefs of this life may we hear his comforting voice as he says, "Be of good cheer for I have overcome the world!"

Be with us, Lord, as we approach the blessed Easter season. As the icy grip of winter is loosened and the brown earth is awakened to life once more, so may the icy grip of greed be loosened from our hearts and we be awakened once more to the life of the spirit. Point our love outward and upward that we may love ourselves as servants of our families, our families as servants of our church and nation, our country as a people called by thee to lead the lands of earth in ways of peace, and all to thy glory; through Jesus Christ our Lord. Amen.

O Lord, our God, we thank thee for the gift of holy habits to keep our lives on the right course. We praise thee for the habit that, week by week, makes us keep this tryst with thee and with each other. Many Sundays we rise from sleep tired from the labors of the week, our minds weighed down with worries, and in our blindness worship seems like a burden. But when we have come to thy house all that is changed, and for this gift we shall give thee humble and hearty thanks.

Here in thy house, our Father, the petty problems of our lives are reduced to size. In the market place the dollar sign is very large and the cross is very small; here the cross is large, and we can rest our eyes upon it. In the hurly-burly of every day our lives are bruised, and we become confused and afraid; here in this place is healing, and one serene purpose, and the mighty power of thy love. The poet has sung, "The fellowship of kindred minds is like to that above," and here, as the wrinkles leave our brows, and the taut muscles of our bodies are relaxed, and the windows of our lives are opened once more to the warm sunlight of thy Holy Spirit, we can believe that he was right. Gratefully we yield ourselves once more to thy fatherly keeping.

O Lord, as we forget ourselves in prayer we remember friends and neighbors to whom this day is one of pain of body or of spirit. Let our prayers reach out to them through thee, giving them strength to endure and courage to overcome. Forgive us the part we have had in creating their pain as we dedicate our lives to making amends for all our sins.

We are aware that as we pray we are part of a mighty world-wide fellowship of Christian prayer. Grant that all prayers offered in Jesus' name may be heard, and that they may form an endless bond of brotherhood reaching around the world; through Jesus Christ our Lord. Amen.

O *thou who art eternal and almighty Goodness,* we praise thee this day for the many ways in which thou dost pour out thy mercy upon us. The food we eat, the clothes we wear, the roofs over our heads, the very air we breathe, all these are tokens of thy grace even as life itself is a gift of thy love. We thank thee.

But thou wast not satisfied with us as mere physical beings and thou dost not stop when thou hast satisfied the needs of our bodies. We thank thee that thou hast made us living souls and hast redeemed us by the sacrifice of Christ. Lest by neglect and sin we miss our highest destiny, do thou remind us daily by the ever present ministries of thy Holy Spirit that we were born to be thy children, nothing less. Fill us with a holy discontent until we have found our peace with thee. As it was with our Master so may it be with us; may our joy be to do thy will.

We thank thee for the power of prayer. All about us and the world around there are lives made whole and beautiful by communion with thee. Let our prayers together this day be an offering of loyalty and dedication to the ends of thy kingdom. Through the invisible waves of thy Spirit let our prayers reach out and touch the lives of each other as we wait in thy presence, and the lives of those near and dear to our hearts who are absent in body from this fellowship, of the needy in body, mind, and spirit in every land, that the flame of Christian love may be kindled in all hearts made cold by fear or sin. And so may our prayers lay hold on thee, and so mayest thou lay hold on us through our prayers that we may be lifted from bondage to the flesh to freedom in the Spirit. We pray in Jesus' name. Amen.

L ord, thou hast taught us that they that wait upon thee shall renew their strength. We come to thee because we need our strength renewed. Some of us have been sorely buffeted by life and need new power to go on in spite of despair. All of us have surrendered to temptation not once, but often. We have not loved thee with our whole hearts, nor have we loved our neighbors as much as we have loved ourselves. We have chosen the easy wrong instead of the hard right and we need strength from on high with which to turn our backs on the sweet, lethal persuasion of evil. Many of us have been blest beyond what is good for us. Instead of being thankful we pat ourselves on the back and take unto ourselves the credit for what thou hast done. We, too, need our strength renewed, strength to strive when there seems to be no need of striving, strength of mind to understand that earthly pleasure is no substitute for heavenly treasure. We wait upon thee, O God, with heads and hearts bowed down. Fulfill now thy promise unto us, that as we go from this place we may run and not be weary, we may walk and not faint.

We pray, our Father, not only for ourselves. Thy whole human family stands in need of the strength that only thou canst impart through prayer. Material power we have in abundance, but it will slay us unless we can find power of spirit enough to master it. So fill thy church with the spirit of the holy cross that there shall be enough to share with those who know thee not. As the ocean moves in upon the shore, slowly by ceaseless attrition demolishing the mighty rocks, so may the rocky hearts of men be melted by the eternal aggression of self-giving Christian love. And give us grace daily to dare to be different because we belong to thee, and wherever it be thy will, use us to accomplish thy purpose; through Jesus Christ, our Lord. Amen.

O God Most High, thy power is a mighty torrent; our power is a trickling stream. Thy wisdom is a flaming torch; our wisdom is a flickering candle. Thy righteousness is like the winter snow, pure and clean and white; our righteousness is like the snow of springtime, gray and soiled and shrunken. Yet One is among us who lived like thee, strong and wise and clean, and at his bidding we worship in hope that we too may share thy Spirit.

O Lord, who hast given us the church and her holy days for our inspiration, we thank thee for the season of Lent. May it be a pilgrimage of recollection as we follow our Lord once more through the days he spent among us: out into the wilderness to do battle with the Tempter, into the market place to ease the misery of the afflicted, up to the hilltop to preach, even up that other hill to die, and on to Joseph's garden there to know the blackness of death and the glorious victory of new life after death; until his life becomes a part of our life, here and now.

Our Father, we praise thee that Jesus sanctified himself for our sakes, making himself holy that we might have knowledge of thy truth and access to thy love. May our worship bring forth good fruits in thought and word and deed. We do not pray for a religion that saves us and leaves the rest of the world to hurtle into darkness, but for such a faith as shall shower blessings far and wide. Let the issue of our prayers be helpfulness and kindness, integrity and uprightness, in every way we walk.

O God, may these days be not only solemn but also joyful. Having found forgiveness for our sins, and hope for our fearfulness, and direction for our striving, may our gladness be as complete as our devotion unto thee; in his name whose meat was obedience and whose drink was doing good, even the precious name of Christ our Savior. Amen.

O *Lord, our God,* each time we worship thee we are stricken by a consciousness of the poverty of the lives we offer thee. We have not loved thee with all our hearts. We have loved ourselves too much and our neighbors too little. The life we live is not like the life of Jesus, and the mind in us is not the mind of the Master. Let the piercing light of thy truth so shine into our lives this day that we shall see ourselves as thou dost see us.

Uncover, we beseech thee, O Lord, all the little falsehoods whereby we lull ourselves into complacency. Prick our consciences awake to the heroic needs of the day in which we live. Set our sights higher so that we may not be satisfied with lives conformed to the standards of this world. We hunger with an appetite that is not eased by anything less than the bread of heaven. Give us, we pray thee, both the wisdom and the strength to live as those who aspire to be thy children.

We pray this day for thy Holy Church Universal. Let the labors of those who would persecute her from without or dishonor her from within be confounded. Let the barriers of creed and practice that keep her members apart be broken down to a height where we can see over them and know that all Christians are brethren in allegiance to their common Christ. May thy church be true to her high calling and her voice be raised against violence and injustice and misery until thy world is at peace.

Be in this fellowship this day, O God, for we have gathered together in thy name. Let this be a fellowship of healing for the downcast, strengthening for the weak, and for all of us one of forgiveness and reconsecration to the great task that is our common mission, even the bringing in of thy kingdom. We pray in the name of Christ thy Son. Amen.

O God of all that is good and true and beautiful, we offer our lives once more to thee in the fellowship of worship. The priests of old burned bullocks on thine altar, but we offer thee no cheap substitutes for ourselves. Here are our hearts. Thou hast made them. Do with them as thou wilt. We recognize and confess before thee that we have marred thy handiwork. Our lives are not pure as we received them, but sullied with sins of both commission and omission. Nothing we can do or say can cleanse them. We can but offer them to thee as they are.

We thank thee for that blessed promise of thine that if we confess our sins thou art faithful and just to forgive them and to cleanse us from all iniquity. We thank thee that through the miracle of thy love to us in Christ Jesus thou canst use even such poor, weak creatures as we are in the wondrous work of thy kingdom; and we bless thy name that daily thou dost open before us ways in which we may be of service to thee.

Take the gift of this hour which we offer thee. Use it to renew our souls. Take from our lives the burdens of doubt and anxiety that weigh them down. Lift us for a few moments above the entanglements of things present that the whole of life in its deepest meaning may be made clear to us. Inspire us with a better acquaintance with Jesus Christ our Lord, and send us forth with him at our side to live and serve in his holy name for thy dear sake. Hear us, O God, for we offer our prayer through the mediation of this same Jesus Christ, our Lord. Amen.

O *Lord God,* we lift up our voices in this hour to join the chorus of praise that never is silent. How glorious it is that as day follows night o'er all the continents of earth, always at any moment there is some place were people join in prayer and praise to thee. Let our worship this day be a link of faith in an endless and unbreakable chain binding us to thee and to one another in holy and victorious love.

O God, who dost will that thy church shall be one even as thou art one with Christ our Lord, we pray for all Christians everywhere. Make us indeed one body together. Let compassion and common faith flow freely from them to us and from us to them, carrying prayers and deeds of sympathy from those who have to those who need. And as it has done in other ages so today may the love of Christians for one another and for thee astound and attract and win estranged peoples to thee.

Merciful Father, who dost know our needs before we declare them yet who dost bid us bring our burdens unto thee, we offer up in thy presence the deep concerns of our hearts. Once more in shame we confess that we have not lived up to the calling wherein we have vowed to walk, but have instead loved ourselves first, our neighbors seldom, and thee hardly at all. Condemn and forgive us, O God, thus granting us the will and the strength to be thy children indeed. We are afraid and proud, bewildered and stubborn. Give us a new heart, we beseech thee, brave and humble, confident and eager, that life may become for us both glad and good.

O God of everywhere and every day, grant us new eyes to recognize thee, not only in thy house, but in our houses, and everywhere we go, in street and shop, in office and in the open countryside. Grant us every moment of our lives to know that in thee we live and move and have our being! To thee be all honor and glory in Christ Jesus forever. Amen.

A *lmighty God,* we praise thee for thy greatness, but we thank thee for thy nearness. The splendor of thy creation, in the midst of which we seem like helpless ants, fills us with awe and wonder. With even greater amazement we find that if we open our hearts to thee after the example of Jesus thou art as close as thou art far, as tender as thou art mighty, as real as thou art wonderful. In fear we bow before our King and Judge, only in love to find thou art our Father too.

Lord of all the nations, we remember before thee thy servants the President of the United States and the Governor of this Commonwealth. We pray for all heads of state, all legislators, all cabinet ministers, and all judges. Enlighten these and all who hold the lives of others under their sway to know that the authority they exercise comes from thee alone. So may laws be made and enforced with such wisdom and justice and love that thy kingdom shall be magnified in the earth.

O thou who art the only God, grant us, we beseech thee, such faith in thee and such love toward thee that our lives may become as whole and single and steadfast as his who is thy Son, our Lord. We are torn asunder, called hither and thither by a hundred different desires and fears. Let one desire take the place of all others, and one great love displace our hundred fears: let the desire to be thy good children be all we want, and let the perfect love of thy Holy Spirit received and given be our joy and inspiration in all good works.

O Lord, since we would have the gifts thou dost impart to thine own people, do thou lay upon us now the tasks which accompany the gifts. We know that holy hopes and joys dwindle quickly when stored up for oneself, but grow a hundredfold when shared with others. Let the treasures of the spirit we receive from thee become a blessing to all whose lives touch ours. We pray in Jesus' holy name. Amen.

1
Passion Sunday

O God, righteous and merciful, who by word and deed hast taught us that there is no greater love than that of him who lays down his life for his friends, come to us as we worship thee on this Passion Sunday, and teach us the bitter, beautiful lesson of the cross. Take us by the hand and lead us to the cross. Take us by the hand and lead us to the hill called "the place of a skull," and show us the terrible cost of human sin.

The people of a dozen nations have been crucified in our generation and we have not been greatly moved. A million children of our time have looked to us from hollow, hopeless eyes and we have thrown them crumbs, appeasing our consciences with a pittance, taking comfort in the thought that they are not our children. But this Man on the cross is our Lord, our Friend who took upon his own innocent flesh the punishment for the sins of all humanity. We cannot close our hearts to his pain. Beat down our indifference by the horror of the cross. Bring us to our knees before the unfathomable mystery of the cross. Reach into our hearts and convert them by the infinite love of the cross, that we, though we may not be able to take Jesus down, may share his mission of grace and partake also by thy mercy in the triumph of his resurrection.

Save us, merciful Father, from lapsing again into the old modes of thought and action after having known the Lamb who was slain. Persuade us to judge all our loyalties by the cross, that we may renounce allegiance to all causes we cannot with good conscience offer to him. Stir us by the death of Christ to a new and deeper self-dedication. So convict our wills and convince our minds that we may all become apostles saying to those we meet, "The hope of men is in him who hung on the tree." Hear us, O God, for we pray in his name. Amen.

2

Passion Sunday

O *God, our Father,* as we remember this day the passion of our Lord Jesus Christ, save us from handling holy things with frivolous hands. Too often when we think of the cross and the events that led to it we take it for granted as something buried in the past. But, Lord, we know this is not so. We know that every day the Son of Man is made to suffer anew by the disobedience and hardheartedness of men. We know that every time we close our eyes to injustice, or sell out to prejudice, or turn our backs on the needs of others, every time we choose to be less than thou madest us to be, if we listen we can hear the reproachful voice of Jesus our Master, "Could ye not watch with me one hour?"

Almighty God, two weeks from this day we would share in the feast of Jesus' resurrection. We would feel the shackles of death fall from our souls, and know the joy of the faithful in all generations who have glimpsed the glory beyond the clouds of time. But, Lord, teach us this day that this victory is not cheap. Before the song of triumph there had to be the battle. Before the mighty soul of Jesus could begin the march of holy conquest down through history, there had to be the sweat-like drops of blood sinking into the cool brown earth of Olivet.

O God, we can ask for no better than our Lord experienced. Weak we are and doubting, but we offer ourselves to thee to be his followers. Thy kingdom come. Thy will be done. Not a thousand years hence, but now, in our midst. Take these lives of ours and rule, for only under thy rule can they be free. Increase the holy fellowship of thy faithful ones until the powers of love and life shall outstrip the powers of hate and death. And of thy mercy keep us faithful, as was our Master, Christ, through whom we pray. Amen.

93

Passion Sunday

O Lord, plenteous in mercy, grant us on this Passion Sunday to know how great a sacrifice thou didst make for us in Christ. Stab our memory with the picture of a cross upon a hill shaped like a skull, called Golgotha, not a pretty cross of gold, but a rough and bloody cross of wood. Take us back to that hill. Let the sword of grief pierce our hearts as it did the heart of Mary. Let us taste the bitter cup of defeat and despair that all the friends of Jesus drank that day. Then when we have that picture etched in our minds, let us bow our hearts in prayer to thee.

We thank thee, Lord, for long years of comfort and joy which, though we did not deserve them, thou didst give us. We thank thee for all fair memories and immortal hopes that are ours because of Christ. We sing hymns of praise to thee because by the pain of Jesus' cross thou didst open a way in the blackness of mortality through which the heavenly light doth shine. Help us to offer the pains and disappointments we have to bear that they may be like the passion of Christ, building stones for the building of thy kingdom.

Fill with the compassion of Jesus his church throughout the world. Stirred by the memory of his glorious life and death and resurrection, may the church of all branches in all lands become his hands and feet and tongue, doing and declaring everywhere the things he would be doing and declaring, never resting while one spirit remains in the darkness beyond his reach. Grant this, O Father, according to thy will, for we pray in his name. Amen.

4

Passion Sunday

O blessed God, we bow in awe as we remember the terrible cost of our redemption in the passion of our Lord Jesus Christ. We remember the agony in the garden, the desertion of his friends, the mockery, the scourge, the crown of thorns, the brutal cross, the cruel nails, the thirst, the pain, the weakness, the death—and all for us. O God, we dare not ask to be worthy of such an outpouring of thy love, but accept our humble gratitude. We thank thee for the unspeakable gift.

We thank thee, gracious Lord, for all the spiritual riches bought for the world by the suffering of our Savior; for that high regard for the preciousness of human personality which has brought about juster laws, more humane institutions, and a thousand movements for the betterment of mankind. Let the pure love of Christ increase until it fills the world and thou art King of earth as well as heaven.

O God of compassion and tenderness, we pray for all who suffer this day: for those in hospitals, and those in countries where there are no hospitals, especially for those who endure with little hope the ills for which no man has yet found a cure. Quicken all impulses of holy compassion. Increase the wisdom of those who seek the sublime gift of healing. And grant to those who suffer a vision of thee that shall impart purpose and meaning to their striving and assurance that whosoever endureth to the end shall be saved.

O Lord Jesus Christ, who wast made perfect through suffering, and who by the discipline of death didst win the victory over death and rise to reign in glory everlasting, grant us a faith like thine whereby to vanquish all fears and doubts and sins that keep us separate from God. So may we walk with thee the way of the cross and find with thee the crown of life. Amen.

1

Palm Sunday

O *God,* whose dwelling is in the infinite reaches of eternity, yet who dost abide in the humble, contrite heart, we come to thee according to our custom to meet in thy presence and to receive a portion of thy Spirit. Fill our minds in these days with thoughts of those other days long ago when Jesus walked among us. Help us to feel once more the tense drama of that last week he was with us as a Man among men. And may the profound lessons of those days of his suffering and death and resurrection be not wasted upon us.

Lord, we believe, help thou our unbelief. Unstop the dry springs of faith in our souls. Give us that trust in Christ which alone can turn our lives wholly toward thee. Thou hast taught us by the stern nature of our time that all the gods of the nations are idols. The strength and wisdom of man are stultified by sin. Give us courage to try in our own lives the real power of love, the real power of prayer, the real power of hope that is in thee. Teach us to trust in thee as a baby bird trusts its mother, in little hops at first and then in longer flights until the sky becomes his home. Thou hast made us for thyself; let us find ourselves in thee.

And having found thee, O God, give us grace to share thee: with those who are lonely and anxious, by the comfort of sympathy; with those who are hungry and cold, by gifts of that bounty vouchsafed to us; with those who know thee not, by thy light shining in us through words and deeds of the kingdom. We pray in Jesus' name. Amen.

2

Palm Sunday

O God, our Father and our King, like the throngs of old who waved palm branches and sang songs of praise at the coming of thy Messiah, so today thy churches are full again of people saying, "Lord, Lord." But we recall that some of those who on Sunday sang "Hosanna" on Friday cried, "Crucify," and we remember with shame that often we, too, have paid our vows on Sunday and blasphemed in thought and word and deed on Monday. Grant unto us this day the grace to praise thee with our whole selves.

O God, as our lips are opened in prayer, so may our hearts be opened to receive thy Holy Spirit. As our voices are raised to sing thy praises, so may our souls be lifted up in devotion to the calling whereby we are called in Christ. As our heads are bowed in worship, so may our wills be bowed to thy will. And as this day we have offered ourselves to thee in faithful words, so this week and all the weeks to come may we offer ourselves to thee in faithful deeds.

As our Lord looked out over his beloved Jerusalem and wept, so we today are moved by deep emotions as we view our community and our world. As we see the seeds of destruction which have been sown in the hearts of men, we look out upon the future with dread. But do thou, O God, arrest this madness. Let faith and hope and love so abound through the power of the cross that the barriers men have erected against each other may be broken down and we may find together the ways of peace. And may this hour spent in thy presence, be to us a time of renewal and a time of high vision, that the empty reservoirs of our spirits may be filled with healing love, and the perplexing questions of our lives may be answered in Christ, through whom we pray. Amen.

3

Palm Sunday

A *lmighty God, our Father,* as we enter this Holy Week we join the throngs who on this day down through the ages have shouted songs of praise, saying, "Hosanna to the Son of David. Blessed is he that cometh in the name of the Lord!" Through long years of halfhearted devotion we have followed many kings. Time was when our delight was in things, our joy was the praise of men, our security was in arms and in dollars. Lord, God of hosts, be with us yet; lest we forget.

Now, O God, amid the shadows of this latter day, while the sons of perdition strive to build a house on shifting sand, while the ashes of former pleasures fly away with the wind, we shout the praise of the only king of men whose empire is everlasting. We remember that he is humble and common, keeping no court, putting on no airs, commanding no armies, approached at will by the humblest of his subjects. Yet the mightiest rulers of the earth are pygmies beside him, for the citadel of his kingdom is the human heart and his authority is the authority of God.

Give unto us, O Lord, the sense of how great a kingdom it is to which we belong. Open our eyes to the vision of the mighty train of his followers, his unarmed soldiers who have "climbed the steep ascent of heaven through peril, toil, and pain." May the fire in their hearts kindle a like flame in our own souls, that this generation may not be without its witness, that the vindication of the faithful may not much longer be delayed.

Remind us, O our God, of the message of the prophet: "Not by might nor by power, but by my Spirit, saith thy God." So shall our trust be placed where victory is assured. So shall our lives fulfill their holy destiny. Hear us, for we pray in the name of Jesus Christ our King. Amen.

4

Palm Sunday

A lmighty God, thy majesty unfolds before us in the orderly march of thy creation. As the first green shoot above the ground is a sure prophecy of springtime's coming, the lowly ride of thy Son into the Holy City is a continuing reminder that the kingdom of love and righteousness will come at last because it is thy will. Hosanna in the highest!

O God, we thank thee for every soul lifted up in worship this day in celebration of the kingship of Christ. May we be of one mind with brown people on South Sea isles who worship in temples with thatched roofs and no walls, with the faithful of China who must worship in secret, with those whose hymns are heard through doors that open on city streets and those who gather in the open country. Make us one people with one holy purpose.

Our Father, grant us the grace of true discipleship that we may learn from Jesus how to live. We are resentful against those who have slighted us, yet he forgave those who killed him; make us like him. We are full of fear though our land bristles with weapons, yet he went forth confidently to conquer riding on a donkey; grant us faith like his. Our lives are full of little compromising self-indulgences, but his is full to the brim of clear, clean love for others. O God, make us thy children indeed.

O Christ, our King, walk very close to us throughout this Holy Week. May our thoughts waking and sleeping be of thee, thy honest open view of what is true, thy faithful ministry in the days when thou didst go about doing good, thy base betrayal and cowardly trial, thy terrible passion and death, thy wondrous resurrection. Make these events in thy life so present that they shall become events in our lives and we may become in fact thy disciples. In thy name we ask it. Amen.

Maundy Thursday

O *God, our Father,* take us back this night to that little upper room where Jesus met to keep the Passover with his disciples on the eve of his death. Open the eyes and ears of our minds that the words that were spoken and the events that transpired there may bring life to our fainting hearts. As the Lord of heaven and earth girds himself with a towel to wash the feet of his followers, may we learn the lesson that humble service is the lot of those who would be great in thy kingdom. As the Master warns that one of us is a traitor, may we like the apostles of old look deep within and say, "Is it I?" and then realize with true penitence that each one of us has played the role of Judas more than once in his life. And then, as the voice of Jesus is lifted up in prayer for us that we may be in the world as his hands and feet, may our souls bow down to receive that holy commission.

There is much in common, O God, between that little upper room and this large one. There were ordinary men faced with a task too great for them, and here, too, are ordinary men and women with neither the strength nor the wisdom to deal with life unaided. But there was thy real presence in Christ, ready to overcome their ignorance with thy wisdom and their weakness with thy power; and here, too, is thy real presence still in sacrament and in contrite heart. Let the Spirit of Christ enfold us and make us one in him, that we may go forth from this place with faith and hope and with high resolve to be in our world as the apostles were in theirs. Take the vows and the covenant here made by all of us, whether for the first time or after many times, and cement them with thy faithfulness, that this hour may be for each one here a commencement, the beginning of a new life so closely entwined with thine that we shall never be apart from thee again. We pray in Jesus' holy name. Amen.

1

A lmighty God our heavenly Father, we bless thy name for the glory that is Eastertide. As thy spring sun melts the ice in the lakes and draws the green out of the brown earth once more, may the warmth of this season renew our lives as well. May the ice melt from our hard hearts so that they will be kind and sympathetic once more. May the frosty crust of cynicism that has so long encased our minds be broken up by the stirrings of thy Spirit within us, and may there blossom once more in our souls those heavenly visions of peace and brotherhood to which we gave ourselves in the days gone by. Let not the message of this day be lost upon us, but may we hear the answer to our deepest longings and our greatest sorrows in the gospel of the risen Christ.

Not for ourselves alone would we pray on this day. We remember before thee thy suffering world wandering in the wilderness of suspicion and sin. May the songs of praise sung this day in a thousand places be heard in the councils of the mighty. May those who guide the destinies of nations become aware that only as rulers are obedient to the King of kings can their reign be assured, and may this day be a new beginning for many in walking the ways of peace.

Together with a mighty company around the world we are met to show forth thy praise, but let us not praise thee with our lips alone. We lift up not only our voices but also our hearts unto thee. Receive them. Transform them. Send us forth into thy world like the apostles of old who were afraid of nothing, not even death itself, because they had seen the Christ of the empty tomb. We pray in his mighty name. Amen.

Eternal God, we are met today as a great company of men and women and children throughout the world to sing thy praises upon the day of days. As the morning sun has shed its light ever westward over the lands of earth it has found everywhere throngs of people gathered to greet the dawn with songs of triumph. We thank thee that we can be part of that great company, and we rejoice in the blessed errand of worship on this day.

Lord, save us from the temptations of the season. Let not Easter be an empty observance of a social custom that goes with the return of springtime. We are Christ's, O God; help us to lay bare our dying, sinful lives to the ever-living Spirit of him who burst the bonds of death this day long years ago. Strike out of our lives all hypocrisy no matter how carefully camouflaged it may be, and make us honest with ourselves.

Our Father, we have tried to enjoy freedom without duty; show us the folly of our way. We have tried to receive forgiveness without true repentance, without being willing to forgive others; show us the folly of our way. We have received without thanks and without giving in return; show us the folly of our way. We have sought year after year to partake of the triumph of Christ's resurrection without being willing to share his cross; show us the folly of our way, and with true contrition may we throw ourselves upon thy mercy.

Teach us, Lord, the impossibility of neutrality in the cosmic struggle of our age between love and hate, greed and compassion. Enlist us this day, each one, in the forces of thy kingdom. Help us by offering our lives to thee to find at last that purpose for which we were born, and give us grace to walk henceforth in the footsteps of the risen Christ wherever they may lead. In his name we make our prayer. Amen.

O God of the living universe, we lift our voices in praise this day for the many signs thou hast given us of the eternal victory of light and life over darkness and death. Every morning thou dost call us back from sleep to a new day full to bursting with living opportunities. Every springtime by miracles we can only dimly understand thou dost bring green life back to the dead brown earth again. And every Easter there breaks upon our ears the song of Jesus' resurrection sung by a million tongues in 1900 springtimes. We praise thee, O living God, for the gospel of life.

O God of all nations and kindreds and people and tongues, we pray for the churchly company of which we are a part. Many we are, and different, full of misunderstandings and blindnesses, jealousies and conflicts, suspicions and evil desires. O God, unite us. As thou art one with Christ thy Son so may we be one in our allegiance to him. Let the common needs of our mortality draw us together to thee, that we may find at thy throne the river of the water of life.

Almighty God, whose nature is powerful love, grant that the worship of thy church today may be such as transforms life. Let each soul be bowed in the receptive humility of contrition. So may faith become contagious, and love leap from heart to heart until the proud are brought low, and the downcast are uplifted, and every life is brought close to that state of blessedness that is thy holy will.

O merciful Father, who dost grant us grace to stand upon the mountaintop of Easter, suffer us not in days to come to forget the vision of eternal hope, but grant that the faith of this day may go with us into every tomorrow, even through all dark valleys we must traverse, that all our battles may be fought on thy side, by thy strength, under the banner of Christ, the Prince of Life, in whose name we pray. Amen.

1

Our Father, we thank thee that thou hast given us to stand upon the mountaintop of Easter. Now that we have descended once more to the round of ordinary days let not the vision be forgotten. For a brief moment the clouds of earth were blown away. For an instant, through the miracle of Jesus' resurrection, we were sure of thy Fatherhood. The deep and beautiful meanings of life were clear and precious. Engrave the faith and hope of Easter deep upon our memory to guard us through the coming months. The downward way before us is dark and perilous. We know not what turn may lead into the valley of the shadow. But empower us ever to see the sun-bathed peak and from it to take our courage for the day.

Give us a religion, O God, that makes a difference. Persuade us that faith that is for our salvation alone is unworthy of Christ, nor can it save us. Go with us to our offices and shops, be in the kitchen and the school, at playground and market place. May the light that shines in our eyes on Sunday be diffused during the week. May our speech be kind and pure, our hands willing and eager, our minds clear and clean, all because thou dost dwell in our hearts through Christ. Thou hast called us to be thy children. Make us discontented with any lesser ideal, nor let us heed the praise or blame of men. Thou art our God; help us to live only unto thee.

Strengthen this thy church with the only power we can rightly use, the might of thy Holy Spirit. Wealth and earthly force we have little, but with thy help we are more powerful than armies. Thy kingdom come, O Lord, beginning with us. In the name of Christ we pray. Amen.

O *Lord, our God,* when we set out to pray to thee we tremble at our audacity. Thou art the Creator of the universe and we are dust and ashes. Yet all the noblest of our human race have lived by the doctrine that thou art a God who hearkens to the prayers of men. With joyful hope we lift our hearts and voices in praise to thee.

O thou great Judge of the earth, how far we have fallen short of the glory that thou didst intend for us. Thou madest us to be noble; we have been petty. Thou madest us to be kind and loving; we have been critical and hostile. Thou madest us to achieve a great zeal for service to thee and to one another; we have a great zeal for our own comfort and enjoyment. O God, forgive us. Restore thy lost image in us. Grant us the grace of true contrition, and plant in us the sincere desire to be noble and kind and zealous.

Father of all mankind, hear our prayers for those whom we love and about whom we are anxious because they live in great dangers to body and soul. Assure them that thou art round about them, and sanctify even their perils to their eternal good. We pray also for those who have wounded us whether justly or unjustly. Since we have found forgiveness in thee, increase our ability to forgive. Grant us wisdom to be firm in the right as we are given to understand it without needing to hate those who disagree with us, and let love crack the walls that divide us.

O God, who didst establish thy church to be the voice of thy Spirit in the world, let us never be content with lives that are merely harmless or no more than respectable. Remind us again and again that each of us is called to be thy witness, proclaiming the good news of our holy religion in word and deed wherever thy providence leadeth us. So may the church be the light of the world shining with the brilliance of Christ, the bright morning star, through whom we pray. Amen.

O Lord, we thank thee for reminding us that we should pray to thee. Our lives are so full of our own little concerns that we would forget thee unless thou didst call us in a hundred ways. This house of worship is thy house saying to us in a voice mute but nevertheless audible, "Pray, for God hears." The books of devotion that lie on our shelves at home, the probing questions of children, the crises of life which come upon us and find us unready, the regular dawning of the Lord's day, all these bear testimony to us as if thy hand stayed us and thy voice spoke: "The hour of prayer has come." In answer to thy bidding we offer thee our prayers.

We thank thee, gracious Father, for all the daily gifts we have accepted from thy hand as if we had made them ourselves. We acknowledge our debt for countless miraculous blessings: for the growth of the seeds in the ground that bring forth fruit for our table, for the steadfast course of our planet earth through space whereby our life is made possible, for the beauties of nature, and most of all the love of God and man.

O God, who by thy great mercy hast made us a thankful church, make us also a faithful church. Keep alive our awareness of churches near and far in all the world to whom we owe brotherly care and service. Open our eyes to see our duty as Christ's own people in this community, and in the state and nation of which we are citizens. Let our association both in worship and in service be radiant with thy light and power.

Mend us, each one, O God, that there may be no weak links in our chain of fellowship. Forgive our blind selfishness. Support us, when we are weak, by thy strength. Grant us spiritual resources equal to our opportunities, and wisdom equal to our tasks, that our lives may be part of the world's health and not part of its sickness. We pray in Jesus' holy name. Amen.

Eternal God, our Father, once more we offer ourselves to thee in the intimacy of prayer. Once more we venture to submit our spirits to the permeating influence of thy Holy Spirit. We know that this will make us discontented with ourselves as we are, that it will create in us a longing after a better kind of life than we have been accustomed to live. But we trust thy promise that when thou hast made us to long after what is wholly good thou wilt satisfy the longing soul with goodness.

In thy presence we remember all those here and throughout the world who have special need of thy grace. Be near to all who suffer: the poor, the hungry, the sick, and those enslaved by evil men or evil habits. By the glorious gospel and by the power of faith strike off the chains that bind men's souls and bodies. Let our prayers reach out also to the indifferent and the lazy, the cruel and the selfish, and when we find ourselves in that number call us back to the way everlasting.

We pray this day for all those in authority in our world: for thy servant the President of the United States, for the leaders of the United Nations, and for all others who hold in their hands the reins of power. Let holy love be stronger than ambition, and the desire to serve be greater than the lust to hold sway, that through these men thou mayest rule by justice and lead in ways of peace.

We have tried, O God, to save our lives, to hoard our hours and our goods for ourselves; but we have found the truth of the saying, "Whosoever would save his life shall lose it." We have seen that the path of selfishness leads only to death. Now we would commit ourselves in trust to thee. Help us to spend our lives with abandon in the service of Christ who poured out his life for us, that true goodness may abound here and everywhere; through the same Jesus Christ our Lord. Amen.

L *ord, God of hosts,* the Almighty, the Creator, the King of the universe, hallowed be thy great and terrible name! To behold thy power, the power that draws the mighty rivers down to the sea, is to be in awe. To contemplate thy glory is to know reverence. And as thy power and glory are great so is thy holiness. To thee be all praise forever and ever.

Our Father, we thank thee for the good news of Jesus Christ who has taught us to believe that at the center of all reality is a heart of love and a mind of infinite wisdom. When we consider our littleness and the vastness in the midst of which we live it is hard to believe such news. Yet when we consider the stature of Christ, and hear his sure testimony, we are led to trust in thee.

O merciful God, who hast promised that when we gather to pray thou wilt be in our midst, and hast encouraged us to bring our burdens to thee as children hurt by the world run home to the sure comfort of good parents, we lift up the concerns of our lives unto thee. We pray for one another and for our church. May our praying together make us better and stronger. We pray for those we love who are far away beyond our protection, or nearby but in dangers over which we have lost control. Be thou their Guard and Defender. We pray for those who belong to this church who are absent because they cannot be here, and for those who are absent because they do not care. Make strong the ties that bind us together as thy people.

We have praised thee, O God, with our lips; send us forth to praise thee with our lives. Grant that we may carry Sunday with us every day of the week, that all our hours may be holy with thy presence and all our tasks, no matter how petty they may seem, may be the stuff of which thy kingdom is built; through Jesus Christ our Lord. Amen.

6

O *Lord, our Creator and our Father,* we have come to worship
thee together. The days of our lives have been full of the
things that hide thy face from us. Our eyes have been focused
upon the clay of which we are made. But today, answering the
still, small voice of thy Spirit that is never altogether silent within
us, we come to thee to offer our devotion. As in the morning
we lift the curtains of our homes to let the sun shine in, so today
we draw back the earthly curtains of our lives to let in heavenly
light and warmth. As we return home to feed our bodies with
rest and food when the day's work is done, so this day at the end
of the week's work we come to thee for spiritual refreshment.
As a child, hurt at play, runs to the comforting arms of his
mother, so do we flee this hour from the buffetings of life to the
everlasting arms of our God.

We thank thee, O God, for the teaching of Jesus that in spite
of our sins we are precious in thy sight, that so great is thy love
to us that each one of us is beloved as if he were the only one
in the world. We come to thee full of shame for the many ways
in which we have failed thee, but we come with confidence, for
we know thou art our Father. Accept our confession of sin as
each of us offers it to thee in his own heart. Take the wounds
we have suffered, whether they be at our own hands or at the
hands of others, and heal them. And turn our thoughts outward
in compassion.

The prayers of this church ascend to thee this day, O God,
for the hearts that are anxious or lonely, for the bodies in pain
and want, and above all for the souls that lie in darkness because
they know thee not. Let our prayers be set before thee as a holy
sacrifice offered in love, and send us forth in thy name this day
with songs of praise upon our lips; through Jesus Christ our
Lord. Amen.

AFTER EASTER

7

O *God,* we thank thee for the many ways in which daily thou dost make thyself known to us. We have heard the whisper of thy still, small voice in the wind about our houses as thou hast sung us to sleep at night. We have witnessed thy power in the majesty of the storm. Thy glorious beauty and forgiveness are in the return of the sun after rain, and of spring after winter. But nowhere art thou so near to us as when we behold thee in the face of Jesus Christ, thy Son. We thank thee with hearts overflowing for the promise of life we have known together in sharing the celebration of his resurrection. O God, let not this experience be wasted within us. May seeds of immortality planted in our souls in this season burst forth into bloom in lives more devoted to things of the spirit, in days more dedicated to service in thy name, in hearts moved to compassion by thy great mercy.

We remember before thee thy holy church throughout the world, and especially this part of it of which we are members. Suffer us never to forget the mission to which we are called, to bear witness in word and deed to the fact that thou has spoken to mankind in Christ and by him dost seek to save the world. Make us, each one and together, good messengers and good workmen for thee.

Our Father, let not thy many gifts to us return unto thee fruitless, but may they make us strong with thy strength, wise with thy wisdom, rich with thy wealth, generous with thy generosity, aglow with thy love, that we from henceforth may be in very truth a people of God unto those to whom thou sendest us; through him whom thou didst send to us, thy Son our Lord. Amen.

O thou eternal God, who dost drape the bare brown arms of the trees with living green leaves each year anew, thou who dost fill the air with the scent of flowers and who callest the song-birds from their nests outside our windows and biddest them wake us in the morning with their carols, we thank thee for the wonder of thy creation. We adore thee for thy gift of springtime.

Hear us, O our Father, as we offer to thee our prayers of thanksgiving: for safe, dry homes in a world where many of thy children sleep in caves; for abundance of good food in a world where many hunger; for good physicians and hospitals in a world where many are born, live out their life's span, and die without medical care to ease their pain or prolong their life; for the blessings of freedom in a world where millions live as slaves; for the wondrous gospel of Christ and the tender fellowship of his church in a world where many have never heard his name save as an evil oath. For these and all good gifts too many to remember, which we own not because we deserve them but because thou art merciful, we thank thee, O God.

Surrounded by the faith of our friends, and bound together by our love for one another and for thee, we offer up our prayers to thee for those who are not here. May our prayers reach out to them as theirs to us, and may they have comfort in our prayers. We pray also for those who are absent because they care not for thee nor for the church. Forgive us when our hardness of heart erects a wall between thy children and thee, and by thy grace charge this house as a magnet which shall pull men by a holy attraction unto thee; through Jesus Christ our Lord. Amen.

A *lmighty God,* our Creator and our King, the Lord of all life, it is thou who hast made us and not we ourselves. We are not our own, but thine. Thy ways are high above our ways as the heavens are high above the earth. Yet, wonder of wonders, thou hast taught us to look up into thy face and call thee Father. For the holy prerogative of worship we thank thee, with amazement and with joy.

Since of thy mercy thou hast come to us in all ages through the great and the good, we thank thee for thy witnesses in all the ages past: for Moses and all the writers of thy holy laws; for Jeremiah and all other prophets who have spoken out for justice and for truth; for Lincoln and all others who gave their days to labor and strive for human liberty; for Pasteur and the great company of those in all times who have brought healing and release from pain to the sick; yea, for all great men and women who in times past have served thee by serving thy people, we thank thee.

Raise up in this great and terrible day, we pray, men and women whose stature is equal to its needs. We pray for all the young in schools and colleges and for those who are their instructors. May the living seeds of leadership and talent which thou hast planted be well and skillfully tended, that those whom thou dost call to be the apostles of this latter day may hear and heed thy voice.

Our Father, we offer our lives upon thine altar. Weak are we all, and often have we failed thee. Yet, do thou take us, O Lord, as we are. Help us to find healing in self-giving. Remake us according to thy holy purposes for us, and send us forth from this place to spread wherever we go the holy contagion of thy love; in the name of him who first loved us, even Jesus thy Son. Amen.

Lord, come and abide with us in this hour. Let the voices of greed be hushed and thy still, small voice of love be heard. Lift up our hearts from the dank sloughs of jealousy, self-pity, and smug complacency. May we fly on wings of prayer to the hilltops of faith and forgiveness from which we can reach out and touch the healing hem of thy garment. May the fears and failures of earth be far removed for these moments while the hopes and triumphs of thy kingdom draw near. May we dwell for awhile in the city that hath foundations, whose builder and maker is God.

Come into our hearts by thy Holy Spirit and give our lives their spring house cleaning. The closets of our souls are cluttered with petty and evil thoughts; take them out, O Lord, and replace them with high and holy thoughts. The windows of our minds are smudged with the accumulated dirt of neglect; clean them with thy gospel so that the light of heaven can shine in. The corners of our spirits are filled with overlooked evil; let the pure wind of thy truth come in to air them out. Let the hot fire of thy judgment descend upon us to burn up the trash. Let us stand before thee like new men and women, clean and free and eager to be thy temples that thou mayest have a dwelling place in the world of humankind.

Hear our intercessions for all who need thee this hour: for those in pain of body and of soul; for those in authority whose decisions shape the future; for those who feel forgotten of thee; and for each other as we worship here, that we may go forth to labor and to pray for the consummation of thy kingdom. Hear us in our Saviour's name. Amen.

May Day

A lmighty and everlasting God, thy greatness overflows every
temple we build for thy dwelling place. No name by which
we call thee can rightly describe thy glory. No image carved by
human craftsmanship, no doctrine fashioned by the mind of man,
can encompass thee who dost encompass all. Yet thou hast made
us to sing thy praise, and that we do, saying with all the prophets
and the martyrs, Holy, Holy, Holy art thou, O God!

Heavenly Father, since by Christ, thy Son, we have been
bidden to pray, do thou teach us to pray aright. For some of us
prayer is a warm glow in the spirit giving comfort and wisdom
for life. For others it is a duty to be fulfilled because we have
been taught that it is right by those in whom we trust. Take us
where we are in our journey, each one, and lift us this day a
little nearer to thee. And in thine own good time grant to each
of us the gift of prayer that is the very giving and receiving and
sharing of the life of God.

On this day which through the years has been marked for
celebrating the rise of labor from weakness to power, we pray
for all men in our world who earn their bread by bodily toil.
Grant unto them wise leaders and true prophets. And grant unto
all of us a brotherly concern that every man shall have a share
of this world's wealth sufficient for his needs in return for his
day's work. Let the dignity of craftsmanship increase, and the
beauty of good work well done be acclaimed.

O Lord, all hours are thine, but this hour we would dedicate
especially to thee. Make us this day more like Christ and less
like that old self with which we are not pleased. When the hour
of worship is over may we not altogether leave thee. As thou
didst bless our coming in, so bless our going out and every way
we travel until the day is done; through Jesus Christ our Lord.
Amen.

Rural Life (Rogation) Sunday

Almighty God, who by the flaming heat of the sun dost warm the cold, encrusted earth until it bursts into bloom, we thank thee for all the wonder and beauty of thy creation which speak to us of thy goodness and thy majesty. We thank thee for the seeds of goodness and beauty and love which thou hast planted in the hearts of men, even our cold, encrusted hearts; let thy Holy Spirit quicken those seeds within us that we may join the flowering earth in reflecting thy holiness.

O thou God of the good earth, we thank thee for all the men and women who spend their lives laboring with thee to bring forth food from the ground. Grant us as we go from this place to sit about the dinner table, a brotherly appreciation for all those whose hard work makes it possible for us to be fed, for those who plow and harrow and plant and cultivate and harvest beneath the sun. Grant them joy in their labor, and a just share of the fruit of their toil. And grant all of us an understanding and a proper esteem of one another as, each in his own place, we do the tasks thou hast assigned us to do for one another, and for thee.

O God of the church, we thank thee for our precious fellowship in this place. Hear our prayers which we offer individually and collectively. Grant us reassurance in presence of our fears, strength of will to ward off both the sudden temptation and the evil habit that would enslave us, and make firm within us our purpose to be true to the covenant in Christ which we have entered into one with another.

O God of love, who hast so loved the world that thou didst give thy beloved Son to save it, do thou grant us, we beseech thee, the greatest gift of all, the gift of thy love, that we may share it one with another and impart it in thy name to those who know thee not. Hear our prayer for Jesus' sake. Amen.

1

Mother's Day

O eternal God, every day of our lives we pray to thee, "Hallowed be thy name." Yet on these same days we defile thy name and worship other gods first: gods of comfort and compromise, gods of convenience and expediency, gods of envy and selfishness, gods of unfriendliness and pride. Almighty God, who by the terrible and inevitable erosion of time hast crumbled all the idols of Canaan into dust, do thou demolish every idol we have set up in our hearts, that we may pray to thee in spirit and in truth, "Hallowed be thy name alone."

Heavenly Father, who hast set the solitary in families, and hast granted to all of us those whom we love and who love us, we come to thee this day with special prayers for all the mothers of the world: mothers in lands plagued with famine and pestilence, whose hearts are broken by the want and suffering of their children; mothers not worthy of their high calling, who neglect their children by failing to pray with them and to teach them that they are thy children; mothers who strive against great odds and amidst great hardship to rear their families in true godliness; and those who are not mothers themselves, yet who love little children enough to take the place of absent mothers. Let the springs of compassion flow freely this day.

O thou great Head of the church, we pray for this church, our spiritual home. We thank thee for the labors of all those who in times past gave of life and love to establish and to preserve in this place a witness to the gospel and a refuge from the storms of history. Make us in truth a family of Christ in that tradition. Strengthen and purify us by our fellowship with him, that in our life and labor thy will may be done; through Jesus Christ our Lord. Amen.

2
Mother's Day

O thou who art from everlasting to everlasting, whose power reigneth over all, on every side we behold the matchless order of thy creation. Let our hearts be lifted up this day to join the rest of the universe in paying thee faithful homage. May we seek the purity of mountain streams, the beauty of opening flowers, the nobility of towering trees, the absolute obedience of the constant stars. And may these treasures once won be our offering to thee.

We offer thee special prayers of thanksgiving this day for all that the word mother means to our world, for all motherly virtues: selfless loving service, pain bravely borne and toil patiently performed, vigilance, tenderness, loyalty, and the imagination that can make even dullness beautiful by the blessing of love. We thank thee for the homes from which we come; in them let the lessons of the gospel be taught and learned and lived, that our homes may be thy home, very outposts of heaven.

We pray, O Lord, for the homes of this nation and of the world: for those where material blessings abound, that the more important spiritual gifts may not be neglected; for those where hardship is felt, that the stern reality of want may knit families together with closer ties of affection; and especially, O our Father, we pray that the good neighborliness taught by Jesus may soon assert itself in the world to the end that no table shall be bare and no hearth cold.

Give us to know that true greatness is to serve thee, true joy is to love thee, and true peace is to know thee, that knowing thee in worship and loving thee in prayer we may serve thee by ministering to one another for thy sake. We pray in the name of him who came not to be ministered unto but to minister, even Jesus our Savior. Amen.

Festival of the Christian Home

O *God,* we recall that when the Lord Jesus Christ chose out of all the words the human tongue can utter the word that should be his name for thee, he chose the word Father, and that when he spoke of his relation to the people of God he called them his mother and sisters and brethren. Receive our thanks for the good and holy gift of the family, and all the tender and precious feelings evoked by thoughts of home.

We acknowledge with shame that our homes, meant to be full of love, are sometimes full of pettiness and hate. Help us, O God, as we set out to be husbands and wives, fathers and mothers, sons and daughters, sisters and brothers, never to forget the holy opportunities present in these blessed human relationships. May the places where we live be kingdoms where love rules, where thy name is revered, where thy Son is always welcome, and where thy little ones can become in very truth building stones for the Eternal City.

As we thank thee, O Father, for the blessings of our family life, we pray for all whose families have been destroyed: for the uprooted and disinherited in all the world; for unloved children deserted by selfish parents; for children whose parents have been taken away by death; for husbands and wives whose love has turned to hate; for all those whose responsibilities are too heavy to bear. We rejoice that though many may be forgotten by men, none are forgotten by thee. Enable the people of God to become the family of the widow and the orphan, that all who have no father may know the love of the heavenly Father.

O God of the church, who hast laid upon us the obligations of brotherhood toward all mankind, grant us no peace or complacency until our household of faith shall be a home for all races, through him who is our Elder Brother, thy Son, our Savior, Jesus Christ. Amen.

Children's Day

O God, to whom we all are as little children, and who art to us the epitome of all that is best in fatherhood and motherhood and more, we come to thee this day to worship thee for the precious gift of childhood. We thank thee for the care with which our parents watched over us in days gone by. We bless thy name for all the love created in the world by the tender relationship of parent with child and child with parent, and we pray for wisdom rightly to understand the coming of thy gift of life.

We remember before thee this day all the little ones of this thy world. We pray for those whose lives have been blighted by catastrophe, that thy Holy Spirit working in us in America may generate a great wave of compassion that shall reach out to them with gifts of sympathy and of faith. We pray for all those in this land of abundance whose lives are being stunted by parental neglect and selfishness. We pray for the children of minority races and downtrodden classes, that the bright hopes of childhood may not be crushed by the intolerant bias of a stiff-necked people. And we pray for the much-loved children of homes where hardship is foreign, that the love of fathers and mothers in these homes may be tempered with wisdom. Grant to all boys and girls in thy world the sure knowledge that they are creatures of thy love, and a redeeming trust in him who long ago called little ones to him and placed his hands on their heads and blessed them.

Grant to all of us this day a new understanding of thy divine Fatherhood. May we capture for ourselves the sincere humility, the sharp curiosity, the unshaking trust in thee of which children are capable. And let us never cease to grow spiritually until we have attained the fullness of the measure of him in whose name we pray, thy Son our Lord. Amen.

1

Memorial Day

O thou almighty God, before whose face the generations rise and pass away, we praise thee that all ages are in thy keeping. We meet to give thee thanks for the inheritance that is ours because of the sacrifice and heroism and faithfulness of those who walk among us no longer. Grant us grace to receive our inheritance as a holy trust from thee.

When the green lawns of our burial grounds are bright with fragrant blossoms, our minds are full to overflowing with things and people and events now woven forever into the fabric of history. As we contemplate mile after mile of white crosses, we bow in shame and penitence that we have not yet learned to walk in ways of peace. For that limitless legion of good servants of thine, those we have known and loved and who loved us even though they knew us well, we give thee thanks. Increase our faith in the communion of saints, that we may have a sure confidence in the ultimate triumph of faithful love.

O God of history, increase our faith in the mighty power of righteousness to prevail. We thank thee that to every generation thou hast spoken through the mouths of men and women, wise and good. We thank thee that the final doom of despots and demagogues is witnessed by the wreckage of their former pomp. We thank thee for the miracle by which the lowly are vindicated at last, and we tremble as we behold the downfall of the greedy. Make us wise to accept the warnings of the past.

O God of all our years, how great and humbling is our debt to the past. Guide and sustain us as we receive this inheritance, defend it, invest it, and share it with the world. And of thy mercy keep us faithful; for his sake who was faithful completely, even Christ, the same yesterday, today, and forever. Amen.

2

Memorial Day

L ord, God of hosts, who markest the rise and fall of nations and of civilizations as but moments on thy calendar, we bow before thee in gratitude as we remember our heritage in this blessed land. We thank thee for all the lovers of liberty on whose devotion this country is built: for the founding fathers who saw the vision of truth that the power of government is derived from the consent of the governed; for wise leaders who took this truth and wrote it into laws and constitutions in the nation and in the several states; for men of war whose blood is the measure of our debt and for men of peace whose lives of service are the planks and bolts and spars of the Ship of State.

Not only the famous and the great would we remember this day. As with the torch of memory we walk the corridors of the past, there come to our minds the faces of those we have known, common men and women like ourselves, even those who in recent time have joined the ranks of the choir invisible; and we give thee hearty thanks for all that they have meant to us, and for the Christian hope by which we expect to walk with them once more in time to come.

On this day, O God, we are deeply conscious that our generation is a link in a great chain of faith that stretches through all ages past and present and future. Enable us, we pray thee, to forge this link so strong that our children and our children's children may lay hold on life eternal. On this day of remembrance let us be so moved by the example of the past that the faith of our fathers may be our faith, and their cause of faith and freedom in fellowship may be our cause, unto the coming of thy kingdom. Hear these and all our prayers, for we pray in Jesus' name. Amen.

Baccalaureate

Almighty God, who desirest that they who worship thee shall worship in spirit and in truth, do thou visit us, we beseech thee, in this our time of prayer, and transform our company into a community of reverent and faithful people. Let the barriers of divergent age and interest and loyalty pale before our common obligation to thee, that as one body we may lift our hearts to thee.

We offer special thanksgivings and intercessions today for the members of the class of ———. We thank thee for their vigorous youth, for their optimism, for their grand vision of a better world and their high hopes that life shall be good. We thank thee for the school in which they have been trained, and for the learning by which they are equipped to render a good account of themselves in the world. Grant them, O Lord, the holy hungers as well as the secular. Enliven in them a longing for the wisdom that is more than knowledge, the hunger and thirst after righteousness that shall give direction to their striving and power to their living.

O tender Father, who lovest each one as if he were the only one in the world, we pray for one another. Sanctify our joys by making us grateful to thee, the Source of all joy. Make holy our sorrows by drawing us closer to thee in the suffering of Christ. Grant us victory over temptation to wrongdoing and steadfast faith by which to endure hardship.

O gracious God, when the hour of worship is ended and we go our several ways, we thank thee that thou canst go with each one of us, and remain with us who stay behind. Grant that the holy Presence which we have found in this place may accompany us all our lives through. Be thou our pillar of cloud by day and our pillar of fire by night, that we, by thy grace, may remain thy faithful people forever and ever. Amen.

O God, who, on that first Day of Pentecost so long ago, didst kindle the fire of thy Holy Spirit at the birth of thy church, help us in this twentieth century of grace to know within our souls the touch of the flaming tongues of heavenly fire. All other power has failed us or turned against us. The ingenuity of our minds has brought forth destruction as well as usefulness. The strength of our own unaided wills is not enough to withstand the temptations of diabolical pride. We have no recourse but in thee, O God. Set us alight that we may be consumed, not by fear and greed and lust, but by thy Holy Spirit of service and love.

On this her birthday we remember before thee thy church, world-wide and eternal, and we pray the prayer of Christ that all her members may be one as thou art one with him. Wherever a simple white spire rises toward the sky, wherever beneath great stone towers or primitive grass roofs the followers of Jesus meet this day to sing the songs of faith, wherever prayers are said in the name of Christ, may thy Spirit be poured out upon the sons of men. Help us all so to dwell on the things that bind us together—our loyalty to Christ, our hunger for salvation, our faith in thee—that the broken body of Christ may be healed.

And we pray, O God, for ourselves met in thy presence. Take from us this day all littleness of vision and give us dreams of thy kingdom. Take from us all the sins we confess and give us the joy of reconciliation with thee. Take from us the hesitancy and reluctance of slothful servants and give us the exuberant loyalty of faithful sons and daughters. Take from us all the burdens of mortality that we, having cast our burdens on thee, may better be able to bear the burdens of others; through Jesus Christ our Lord. Amen.

A*lmighty God,* on this the anniversary of her birth we remember before thee thy holy church. We deplore her sinful divisions, her coldheartedness, her lack of devotion, and we bow in sorrowful penitence that these faults are our faults, for we are thy church. But we bless thy name that in spite of her faults thou hast made her thy dwelling place. Stir us lest we miss the meaning of worship. Let no one of us come to this meeting and go away not having felt thy presence with him in his heart. Let the fellowship we know together be fraught with the kind of power of which new lives are made and old lives are changed for the better. And may this church, living as it does, in the world yet on the edge of heaven, be an open door for thy entry into our lives and our society.

Let this thy church be a refuge for the hard-pressed. May those who have come with problems greater than they can handle alone, find here both the way and the power by which to overcome. But grant, O God, that this church may be more than a place of spiritual rest and healing. Imbue our fellowship with such a love toward thee that our whole lives, at home, at play, at business, and at labor, may become fragrant with thy grace; that we may be not only receivers of thy mercy but transmitters as well, that through us others may be led to thee.

And may our prayers go out this day to touch our fellow Christians to the north and the south and the east and the west. Increase the sense of brotherhood that we have with other followers of Jesus, white or black or brown, wise or foolish, rich or poor. So may our sense of oneness increase that we may be cords binding together the brokenness of the church until, made new again by peace within, she may better carry on the struggle for peace without among ~~the sons of~~ men; in the name of Jesus Christ, our Lord. Amen.

Pentecost Communion

A*lmighty God,* our Creator and our King, great and marvelous are thy works; just and true are thy ways. Thou art at home in the far reaches of space beyond our vision and our ken; thou art equally present in the midst of the tiny atom. We have lifted up our voices in songs of praise; do thou lift up our hearts in loving adoration, for we are met to worship thee.

In this hour when we wait before thine altar, we are freshly aware of how great a family it is of which we are members in thy holy church. We thank thee for saints and martyrs, for prophets and pilgrims of the past, and also for that great company of all races and nations in our day who own our Lord as theirs. Let the bonds of love for one another and the mutual loyalty to the Lord Jesus which bind us together be a bulwark of peace and a beacon of hope.

O thou Defender of the defenseless and Father of the fatherless, hear our prayers for all those who this day have special need of thy holy help: for the leaders of the nations; for all legislators and statesmen who are criticized for holding fast to what they believe is right and good; and for all those in any arena of politics or social turmoil who put their trust, not in the righteousness of might but in the mightiness of right. Be thou their God, as thou hast been their fathers' God.

Since thou hast promised to make the humble and contrite thy dwelling place, abide with us as we bow in prayer. Replace our fears with faith, our pride with thankfulness, our hardness of heart with Christian compassion, and our weakness of will with steadfastness. And to thee be all the glory, world without end; through Jesus Christ our Lord. Amen.

Pentecost and Memorial Day

*O*ur *Father,* we thank thee this day for the halls of memory wherein we may walk by the turning of a thought. Inspire us by the lives of those who have fought the good fight in other years. We see the crosses, row on row, that mark the place of all that is earthly of those who have guarded the ramparts of liberty. We are made mindful of the great price at which freedom is bought, and we offer thanks to thee for the inheritance of which we are not worthy. Teach us, Lord, that freedom must be exercised as well as defended, and help us, by zealous use of the precious privileges of democracy, to keep them strong and vital.

We bless thy name this day for all that cloud of witnesses in heaven who have been the soldiers of thy kingdom since the days when Jesus walked the earth. Many there are who have "climbed the steep ascent of heaven through peril, toil, and pain." Others, and among these are many near and dear to us, have only done the day's labor with patience, cheerfulness, and love. But we thank thee, Lord, that all are precious in thy sight and safe in thy hands forever.

Let the same Holy Spirit who came into the world through the hearts of those early disciples of Jerusalem dwell mightily with us in this crucial time. Crack the tough shell of sloth and greed by which we have imprisoned him within us, that his light may flood our whole life with light, and that such power for good may be released in thy church that no man will be able to say, "I have not heard of the gospel of Christ." Together with the faithful of all ages, may we glorify thy holy name, and thus find our salvation; through Jesus Christ our Lord. Amen.

Trinity Sunday

*L*ord *of the universe,* thou who dost steer the flaming sun through the sky, who callest the waters of the sea back twice each day to wash the shores of the land with great tides, thou who art the Creator of our earth and all the whirling worlds whose shining paths in the night do make us marvel, thou cunning Craftsman who dost fashion the snowflake and the cedar bough and the restless fingers of the human babe, how is it that we crass creatures of earth dare pray to thee? O Lord, our Lord, how excellent is thy name in all the earth!

O thou great Governor of all the lands of earth, hear us, we beseech thee, as we pray for the nations and for our nation. We pray for the President of the United States and for the Governor of this Commonwealth. We pray for the representatives of the world's peoples who gather in the United Nations to seek together the way of peace. Guard and guide them all, we implore thee, that they may have such a concern for the people they serve that all personal ambition and national pride may be forgotten in a life-consuming devotion to the ideal of a world made one under thy laws.

Our Father, who dost greatly love us all, may we be comforted and uplifted by each other's prayers. Meet, we beseech thee, the special need of each one of us—for chastening and repentance, for renewed faith and hope, for a purpose in living, for the strength to go on a little longer, for a thankful heart in the presence of thy mercy.

O Lord, grant that this hour may be fixed in our memory as a joyful and a holy time. May the warmth of it shed a glow upon the days ahead, to guard us from stumbling, to give us serenity in the midst of the world's clamoring confusion, and to guide us that we may wander neither to the right nor to the left from thy straight path; through Jesus Christ our Lord. Amen.

1

O God, so mighty yet so merciful, to whom angels and archangels continually do cry, singing Holy, Holy, Holy, thou who knowest even the thoughts of our inmost hearts better than we know them ourselves, give us, we pray thee, met here in the spirit of worship, that assurance of thy presence promised to those who gather in thy name. As we join in silent communion with our friends and neighbors in the fellowship of thy church, may it be given us to know that that fellowship is vertical as well as horizontal, that the deep yearnings of our hearts are heard even before they are uttered.

We thank thee for all things vouchsafed unto us as thy children: for the ordinary necessities of life by which our bodies are preserved; but more for those unseen treasures of the spirit, for faith, and hope, and love, and for the glorious gospel of Jesus Christ by which we live and of which we need not be ashamed. Set our hearts ever more firmly in pursuit of true pearls of the kingdom, that the trash of this world may not divert our lives from thee.

We remember in thy presence all those in our fellowship who are lonely and anxious, those homes where the angel of death hovers near, all those who are ill or in pain. Attend thy suffering children, O God, in all the world, and use us all as instruments of thy compassion.

We pray for each other. Some have come here with deep troubles to face; do thou lead them out of the vale of trouble. Some have come here living in the grip of temptation to evil; free them from the chains of wrong desire. All of us have sought thee here with sins to confess and weak lives to be strengthened. Do thou forgive, and give us such faith in thee that together we may sing the songs of victory; through Jesus Christ our Lord. Amen.

A *lmighty God,* who, in seeking life for thyself didst find that life in giving, we cry to thee from this vale of trouble, "Help us likewise to find life!" We praise thee that from the beginning of creation thou hast not withheld any good thing from thy creatures. After thou hadst breathed into man the breath of life, thou gavest him all things needful to preserve life, opening the endless treasures of earth and bestowing upon him fruit and flesh to eat, minerals, textiles, and woods for his comfort. And when the soul of man languished in death thou didst stint not, but didst send forth the unspeakable gift, even Jesus Christ our Lord, that in him we might find the victory over sin and death. Thou gavest of thyself to us, O Lord, that we might learn the lesson that abundant living is self-giving.

Weak though we are, by thy mighty power make us able to live aright. We long for friends; increase within us the capacity for friendly acts. We would succeed in our chosen occupations; increase within us the capacity for the task well done. We would know the radiance of a life lived at peace with thee; increase within us holy compassion, divine concern, that our souls by pouring themselves out may become clear and pure. Make us channels of thy grace, that having richly received of thee we may render unto others that which thou hast given us, and so find the holiest joy of all, that of being useful in thy kingdom.

To this end, O God, make us much aware of our Master, Christ. Let us walk daily with him in prayer, in work, in service, in joyful fellowship with the companions of the way, in life that is good because it is with thee. Hear us, O God, for we pray in his name. Amen.

Jun 12-64

Almighty *God,* our Creator and our Governor, we meet to praise thee by the lifting up of our voices and our hearts and our lives to thee, the Father Everlasting. Great and marvelous are thy works. Thou dost call the mighty rivers down to the sea, yet thou dost also guide the tiny tendrils of the climbing vine into the crevices of the wall. And it is thy wondrous providence that marks a pathway through the sky to lead the migrating bird to its home again. O God, hear us as we join thy whole creation in psalms and vows of adoration.

adlib on this
O thou great God to whom we owe each breath of our life, we thank thee for the joy of thanksgiving. Since thou hast surrounded us with countless tokens of thy love, it would be a thing hard to bear not to be able to pour out our gratitude in return. For the light that shines in the laughing eyes of children, for the handclasp of a good and faithful friend, and above all for the love that came into the world in Christ and resideth still in the church, we give thee thanks.

O gracious Father, hearken to us as we remember before thee all those who have need of thy mercy. We pray for one another, for our church and its ministry to this community. We pray for those dear to us whose names thou knowest, who are in danger, or in pain, or in the midst of trials of body and soul. Especially do we pray for those who know not how to pray for themselves.

O omnipresent God, as thou hast filled this hour and this place with thy nearness, go with us every hour of this week, erecting barriers of judgment across every evil path we are tempted to enter, guiding us by thy holy laws in every good work to do thy will, for so alone may we fulfill our hearts' desire to be thy people after the perfect pattern of Jesus Christ thy Son, in whose blessed name we pray. Amen.

4

Gracious God, we come to thee this day with gratitude for thy great undeserved goodness to us, for the beauty of the season that speaks to us of release and rest and pleasanter labor, for the thrill of the seedtime with its promise of new life to come, for thy voice in the wind and thy smile in the sun and thy riches in the gentle rain. Even more we thank thee for these very lives we live by thy grace, and for those other lives we love and that love us, and most of all for the hope set before us in the gospel of Jesus that life is eternal victor over darkness.

We remember before thee especially this day all young people who have come to the time of their graduation from schools and colleges. May the hour of joy they share with those who love them and who have sacrificed so much for them be an hour of true gratitude as well. May the hopes they have for a happy future be untarnished by selfishness, and may their ambition be redeemed by the desire to serve thy people and thee in honorable work. Give them the twin graces of persistence and courage, that whatever they begin that is good they may finish to their growth and thy glory.

Help us, O Lord, to use all hours to the upbuilding of our lives. Let hours of hardship minister to fortitude, and hours of peace and joy to strength of soul for darker days. May times of want teach us thrift and self-denial so that times of plenty may not be wasted. And let all times be great with compassion for those who suffer and with devotion to the high calling whereby we are called in Jesus Christ. May this hour of worship and all hours spent in thy presence be for the cleansing of our hearts, the quickening of our minds, and the peace of our souls. We pray in Jesus' holy name. Amen.

Almighty God, Soul of the universe, Author of life, we thank thee for that in man which has led him in all the ages to seek thee in worship. In years of quiet peace and years of war and pestilence, in climates desert hot and icy cold, at all times and in all places the sons of men have sought to make their peace with God. And so do we.

Thy ways, O Lord, are high above our ways as the heavens are high above the earth. We are incomplete and earthy, weak and imperfect, full of prejudice and jealousy. Yet through the teaching of prophets and apostles and by the grace of Jesus we dare to aspire to become complete and heavenly, strong and perfect, full of honesty and love. This can never be our achievement, and will come only as thy good gift, given in thy way, at thy chosen time. Therefore we yield our lives to the sway of thy Holy Spirit.

O Lord, thou God of hosts, we offer prayers this day for our nation and our world, for all the people thou hast made to live upon the face of the earth. We behold with dread the rising tides of suspicion, fear, anger, national pride, and unholy ambition which threaten to engulf us once again in orgies of killing. O Father of mankind, let the voices of patience and peace, of friendship and forgiveness, be raised and heard and heeded in the councils of the nations. Spare us from war by making us worthy of peace.

O God, who dost give us in this place and this hour a glimpse of things eternal and holy, send us back to the everyday world more eager to do thy will and less eager to vanquish our fellow men. Lift the goals of our lives to new and higher levels. Make us thy people, able to live as well as to pray in the name of thy Son our Savior, Jesus Christ. Amen.

6

O eternal God, who alone canst see the end from the beginning, we thank thee that here in the darkness of this world of sense where all is uncertainty and chaos we can still reach out in prayer and, touching the hem of thy garment, know thou art near. We are grateful that no matter what terrors or disappointments we may be called upon to face, thou art our Father and all else pales before that great fact. We rejoice that in bright days and dark we may have sure confidence in the everlasting compassion of the Most High.

We bless thy name, O Lord, for the good gifts which have flowed so freely from thee to us all our days. Thou hast given us homes to share with those we love, food and drink for our life, shelter and clothing for our comfort, the joys of a beloved community where people are friendly and are concerned for one another. All these thou hast given without our asking, and many times without our gratitude. For all thy bounty we offer thee this day our belated but heartfelt thanks.

Since we cannot face thy goodness to us without being painfully reminded of the terrible needs of others, we open our hearts this day to the call of thy compassionate Spirit. We pray for all of our fellow citizens both young and old who have been stricken with the scourge of dreadful disease. Strengthen thou the hands of those who would help them. And we remember all thy children everywhere who are hungry or cold or in pain, lonely, fearful, or anxious. May the reservoirs of divine love be unstopped and the healing streams of mercy cover the earth with good neighborliness.

And dedicate us here this day to the tasks for which thou hast chosen us. We have no strength, no righteousness, no wisdom of our own. But do thou renew our lives by thy strength, thy righteousness, thy wisdom unto our salvation and thy glory; for Jesus' sake. Amen.

7

O *thou who didst fashion the planets and the stars* and whose wisdom designed the human soul, we enter thy presence this day in search of life. We acknowledge in thy house our utter dependence upon thee for each breath that we breathe. From everlasting to everlasting thou art God. In the beginning thou wast the Creator. Every day thou art the only true Guide, the only sufficient Power. And in the end thou art our only Savior. We place our trust in thee.

Thou hast given us to live in a dark valley of history, O Lord. All about us is foreboding darkness. But it is still thy world and we are still thy people. Lift us by our prayers to a height from which we can see things whole, not just the little bog in which our feet are mired. As the world of sense is more and more covered with peril and confusion, strengthen our hold on the eternal world of thy kingdom. Teach us that with Jesus by our side we can go in no direction save toward thee.

Our Father, we thank thee for the gift of life, for talents of hand and mind, of eye and ear. Lead us aright as we seek to strike our blows for thee where they will do the most good. We know that he who truly loves can do no wrong. Do thou therefore cleanse our hearts of all selfishness that we may have room for thy compassionate Spirit. So enflame us with eagerness to serve that all fears may melt away.

Since thou hast called us together to be thy church in this place, make us fit for thy calling. Let our warm friendship for one another as fellow Christians be such as will make others want to share it. May cordial hands of fellowship and service reach out from this meetinghouse into every place of loneliness and of need that the healing, saving work of Christ may go on. And since we have no power of ourselves to do thy will, do thou supply us, and to thee be all the glory; through Jesus Christ our Lord. Amen.

O *thou in whom we live and move and have our being,* our Father and our God, often when we look to thee in worship words fail us. Nothing we can say aptly describes the wonder of being with thee. All words seem weak and empty and futile. Yet thou hast taught us to pray without ceasing, and dost assure us that the most high God taketh pleasure in the prayers of men. For this we give thee thanks.

O Lord, we praise thee for the marvels of our modern world. We thank thee for the inventive genius of thy creature, man, whereby our comfort and convenience are so miraculously served. We praise thee for the radio and the airplane, that have made of our world a neighborhood. And for all the skills and drugs and apparatus of the healing art that lengthen life and free it from pain, we do thee honor. Especially we pray for all men of science that they may not lose touch with thine eternal laws, that the inventive genius so full of blessing may not be allowed to turn and destroy us.

O God, by the power of prayer we would let loose upon the world the healing of thy presence. We remember before thee those whom we know who are ill or in pain or trouble of body, mind, or estate. For these, and for those others whom we know not who need thee just as much, we pray. Be round about them in their hour of testing. Make it for their good and not their harm.

And receive, O Father, our confession of guilt. We have not loved thee with all our heart and soul nor with all our mind and strength. We have not enough loved our neighbor as ourselves. We have transgressed thy laws both known and unknown. Yet we throw ourselves on thy mercy. Blot out our sins by thy forgiveness that we may become channels of thy grace in a needy world; and thine be the praise and the glory. Amen.

9

O God, whose greatness is the greatness of the universe and whose tenderness is like that of a Father, we lift up our hearts to thee this day in worship. Thou art great; we are weak. Yet we praise thee that thou didst love us enough to make the souls of men thy dwelling place. Cause us to know in this hour that thou art our God and we are thy people.

We thank thee for all the things for which in other days we have forgotten to thank thee: for glorious autumn days when the valleys and the hillsides shout thy praises with gorgeous colors; for daily bread and all the other necessities of the body that thou dost provide; for the love of those near and dear to us; for the loyalty of good neighbors and friends; for memories of the good past and for the eternal hopes set before us in the gospel; for thy mercies freely outpoured.

We thank thee for the place of labor thou dost give us in thy kingdom. Though some of our daily tasks seem dull and cumbersome, they are of vital importance when we do them to thy glory in love. We labor not only for ourselves and our families, but for the establishment and extension of thy kingdom where we live and throughout the world. Thy kingdom come, O Lord, beginning with us.

Give us a glimpse in these moments of worship of things eternal. Help us as we study the life of our Lord Jesus Christ and listen to his words to understand the meaning of life as he understands it. Take away our pleasure in evil things and set our hearts upon true and eternal joys. Increase our hunger and thirst for righteousness. Make us long above all else for the heavenly gifts of faith and hope and love. And then satisfy our hunger, we pray thee, by sending us on thine errands. Take our labors and our pains and our prayers and consecrate them to thy glory and our salvation, for his sake who died that we might live. Amen.

O *Lord, our Lord,* how excellent is thy name in all the earth. When we consider thy heavens, the moon and the stars which thou hast ordained, we are constrained to ask, "What is man, that thou art mindful of him, or the son of man that thou visitest him?" Yet thou hast made him a little lower than the angels and hast crowned him with glory and honor. Thou hast put all things under his feet and given him dominion over the work of thy hands. For this we praise thy name.

O God of mercy, who hast not rewarded us according to our iniquities, we bow before thee in humble contrition. How great is thy goodness to us, and how feeble and unfulfilled are our good intentions toward thee. Since we have no power in ourselves to save ourselves, do thou grant us thy Holy Spirit, that we may love thee as we should. Let thy love for us be magnified in our love for one another. Fill us with a holy discontent with anything less than a faithfulness to thee that is like thy faithfulness to us.

Our Father, who dost know us better than we know ourselves, hear our prayers for others. Particularly do we pray for all who bear the burdens of great responsibility in our world and nation. We pray for presidents and prime ministers, for governors and ambassadors, for the captains of labor and of industry. Speak to their hearts in the quietness of the night, that they may hear the word of the Master of all men: "Blessed are the peacemakers, for they shall be called sons of God."

O Sun of the whole universe, be the God of all our lives, not just our Sunday God or our Christmas and Easter God, nor only the God of our time of trouble. Fill our waking and our sleeping, our work and our play, our times of peace and of pain, until our lives are as full of thee as the oceans are full of sea; through Jesus Christ our Lord. Amen.

11

O *God, our Father,* whose presence is a holy joy to them that love thee, we meet to worship according to the custom of our fathers. Age after age the sons of men have sought thee in every time of trouble and of joy and without fail have found in thee all the necessities of life and of death. We of thy church are a diverse company, O Lord. We come from many nations, from all classes, young and old, men and women and children; but we are all one in our common humanity and in our common need of thy salvation. Speak to each of us the word that he needs, and let thy word abide with us until it has wrought in us thy holy will.

We come to thee, O Lord, bringing our great needs to thy great mercy. All of us are anxious; restore in our hearts the realization that thou art our Father God, that our anxiety may be driven out. All of us are weak; renew in our souls the power with which to resist temptation and the desire to do that which is good and holy in thy sight. All of us are infirm in body, mind, or spirit; reach into our lives with thy healing fingers and touch us that we may turn toward wholeness again. All of us are half-hearted; kindle again the fires of enthusiasm for all good causes, that we may go forth once more to do battle for thee against the powers of ignorance and sin.

Hear us, Lord, as we pray for all who need thee more than we do: for the aged and the sick who would be with us if they could, and for those who know not the way of worship, that thy Holy Spirit who doeth all things well may be their comfort wherever they are; for those who groan beneath the burdens of physical hardship, that the hearts of the more fortunate may be moved to give them succor; and for all who are in any wise afflicted. Let our prayers go out with power unto the coming of thy kingdom and the salvation of all thy children; through Christ our Lord. Amen.

O thou mighty God, who art our refuge and strength, we thank thee that thou hast led us to this place. We come from a world where life is cheap; here it is more precious than gold. Sometimes where we work we are given to understand that we are merely units of production or cogs in a machine; here we are thy children and thou art our Father. In the confusion of everyday living sometimes we lose our sense of direction and it seems as if life were a blind alley leading nowhere; here we are face to face with a destiny that is greater than this world can hold. In the world of commerce and politics things loom very great and people very small; here in this place where the memories of the centuries crowd around and where the cross of Christ is elevated before us, we know that in all thy creation human personality matters most.

O God, who hast given to us the holy heritage of humanity, save us from complacency at being less than what thou madest us to be, that we who were made to share the glory of the saints may never rest until the mind of Christ is ours. As the days and years go on let the joys we have in things that die decrease, and let the spiritual sensitivity that ties us to thee increase until our hearts are surely fixed where true joys are to be found. May we line the treasure houses of our souls, not with the bric-a-brac of worldly trinkets, but with the lasting wealth of friendship, sturdy principles, high ideals, and noble endeavors completed in thy name.

Let this hour spent in thy presence be a rest along the way of life. We lay here before thee all the unnecessary baggage we have been carrying, all fears and cares, even our anxiety for those we love since they are in thy hands, all the beloved sins we have cherished hitherto. May we rise and go from this place as those who go refreshed upon a journey with a Beloved Companion, even Christ Jesus, our Lord. Amen.

A Day of Trouble

O Father, much there is in life that vexes us and which we cannot understand, yet more there is of the good and the holy and the beautiful. Help us in these moments to turn away from the darkness and look unto the light. We thank thee for the many days we have known that have been happy days. As we look back over the years sometimes we are full to overflowing with thankfulness. We bless thee for those unexpected and undeserved acts of kindness in time of need which we have received from good neighbors and friends and loved ones. We thank thee for successes, small and large, which thou hast granted unto us; for satisfaction we have had in tasks completed with thy help. And for all those myriads of gifts of thine which we have known and forgotten, we thank thee.

When we consider thy great mercy we can turn to the daily battle against evil with greater courage, in the knowledge that for the Christian there is never a day when the faith in a better tomorrow need falter. In this hour of meditation upon the holy sacrifice of Jesus we see our burdens and problems, petty by comparison, as parts of a great crusade of redemption. We offer unto thee this day the burdens thou hast given us to bear. Do thou sanctify them and use them to the easing of the hardships of those less fortunate than we are.

Lord, grant that our prayers may reach out through thee unto all homes where evil reigns. Take courage and hope to those places where there is fear and despair. May sympathy be converted into groceries and clothes for those who are hungry and cold. And wilt thou ordain us all to be evangelists, that no one may live and die without hearing of Christ and his gospel. We pray in his holy name. Amen.

1
Election Sunday

O Lord, the Father Almighty, before whose face the generations rise and pass away, the Beginnning and the Ending, our Source and Destiny, from everlasting to everlasting thou art God. Caught in the narrow vale of the here and now, our eyes are blinded by the turbulent events of this day and this week. Lift us in worship out of ourselves that we may see today in the holy perspective of forever. So may we be able to see our world in our day truly, as thou dost see it.

We offer prayers of intercession for all the peoples of the world who have been forced by the rashness of an angry few into the perilous shadow of war. Let thy guiding Spirit be with all who seek peace, that no opportunity may be missed to end the folly of bloodshed. O God, let the compassion of the world be increased by the sufferings of the little people who are the innocent victims of other men's malice, and may such an outcry of righteous revulsion be raised that those who have taken the sword will be moved to sheathe it before it is too late.

O Lord of nations, we pray for our country in the day of voting. Let the decision of the people be the one that is pleasing to thee, and when the day is over and the decision is known let all the hot words of the campaign be forgiven. Then let the devout prayers of all Christians be lifted up to thee for the candidate who shall be chosen as our next President, whoever he may be, that we may be one people again.

O God, who hast granted us the wondrous privileges of worship together in thy church, let the Spirit we have encountered here follow us wherever we go—to our homes, our places of labor, our places of pleasant fellowship, everywhere—that no hour of our life may be lived apart from thee. We pray in the name of Christ, thy Son. Amen.

2

Election Sunday

Almighty God, it is thou who hast made us and not we ourselves. The wondrous pageant of thy creation surrounds us in the autumn. Our eyes are fed on the splendor of sky and scudding cloud and gorgeous hillside. The scent of burning leaves is in the air and when we listen we can hear the *au revoir* of birds departing for the winter. All these are thine, O God, and so are we. Therefore, in grateful awe we worship thee.

O God, grant us grandeur of soul equal to the grandeur of thy universe. When we turn from worshiping thee to look inward upon ourselves, our meanness is more mean for the contrast. The grudges we nurse, the hardness of heart in the presence of the great needs of our fellow men, the miserable pride we feel at such a little bit of righteousness, all the selfish passions that consume us when we were meant to burn with holy love for thee —these bring us to contrite shame. Convert us, O Lord, lest our lives sound off key when all creation praises thee.

Lord God, we offer special prayers for our nation as we enter the valley of decision once more to choose a President. Grant us, though this be a hard boon indeed, both zeal and compassion. If we belong to one party it is hard to understand how Christian men can belong to the other. Yet they do. Let all our striving against one another be in love and in the light of the truth of the gospel. And when the campaign is over and the choice is made, let all who call themselves Christian be united in dedication to the common welfare.

Almighty God, Father of our Lord Jesus Christ, who hast taught us by him that we, too, were made to be thy children, quench the fiery desires that lead us downward to less than manly deeds, and fill us with holy desires that we may go forth to work the works of God. We pray in Jesus' holy name. Amen.

Reception of Members

O thou who art from everlasting to everlasting, God of the smiling sun and the pouring rain, Creator of the hurtling planets, Spirit of the sea and the forest and the blaring, teeming city, how poor do our words seem when we offer them to thee in prayer. Thou art so great and we are so small. Yet there is within us a yearning that cannot be silenced save as we pray to thee; and so we turn away once more from our striving to offer up our lives to thee who made them.

Eternal Father of all mankind, who in every generation hast gathered from the world men and women to do thy work and bear thy tidings, we remember with awe that we are thy church for our time and our place. Nothing have we done to merit this holy assignment. Nay, in many ways we have shown ourselves unworthy by selfish pride and faltering zeal and unfulfilled promises. But thou art God, who makest even the wrath of man to praise thee. Endow us with a new spirit fit for a new day.

O God, look with favor upon those whom we have received into our communion and fellowship. Help them to live up to the vows they have taken, and help us in steadfast love to be worthy of their high vision of what this church should be. Let our worship together in the weeks and years ahead glow with the warmth generated by thy living Spirit, and let the influence of our association with one another and with thee be felt to the ends of the earth for good.

And when we have sung thy praise and offered our petitions and heard thy word, go with us as we return to our homes and the places where we labor. Be beside us all the week long, that wherever a member of this congregation shall be, there thy gospel may be preached in life; through Jesus Christ our Lord. Amen.

Installation Sunday

A*lmighty God,* on this day when we install the officers who will lead and serve us in the coming year, we remember before thee this church. We thank thee for all the good people who, year by year, have had its prosperity and peace upon their hearts. We have entered into their labors and acknowledge our debt to them. We thank thee for the increase which thou hast granted us in these years of our fellowship together, and we bless thy name for the many gifts of thy mercy, and for the many works begun, continued, and brought to completion in thy providence.

Be with us as we face the future. Overcome its darkness and uncertainty with the light of thy countenance and the knowledge that the hour of serving thee is ever present. Increase the bonds of affection that bind us one to another as a church. Let our mutual loyalty to Christ and his kingdom outweigh any of the differences of opinion or status that would tend to keep us apart. Help us to unlock the infinite resources of thy Holy Spirit. Kindle our lives with fire from on high, that we may not only be purified and strengthened to withstand the onslaught of temptation and adversity, but may so bear witness to thy presence in our lives that others may desire thee also.

As thou didst call and commission Paul of Tarsus long centuries ago to serve and to witness as an apostle, do thou commission us this day to the fulfillment of our stations in thy holy church. If we be appointed leaders, give us true vision and great humility. If we be among those who serve, give us great devotion and loyalty. And to all who follow thee in whatever way grant the great joy of belonging to the part of human history that is eternal; through Jesus Christ our Lord. Amen.

Church School Installation

O *Lord, Jesus Christ,* who wast called Teacher when thou didst walk among men, we thank thee for the blessed work of communicating the truth of the gospel. We bless thy name for those people in all churches across the land who dedicate the powers of their minds and their inmost selves to the ministry of teaching.

Particularly, O Lord, we commend to thy care those who this day take up their duties as teachers and officers in our church school. Remembering that all Christians are priests called to special ministries, we give thee thanks that thou hast awakened in these our friends a desire to give themselves to this holy endeavor. Grant them wisdom equal to their tasks and devotion commensurate to their opportunities. May they not only teach their pupils, but also love them, and may their goal be to inspire as well as to inform. Let their faith be of the kind that is caught as well as taught, and may their reward be found in lives made new by the grace of the Holy Spirit.

Be round about all of us in this church, O Lord, that the task of teaching may not end when these, our leaders, have ceased to teach for the week. Let the homes of this parish be an extension of the church school, and let the lessons learned here be reinforced both by precept and example in the places where we live and labor and love; through Jesus Christ our Lord. Amen.

Homecoming Day

O *Lord,* how marvelous a thing it is to pray. Life is full of many things. We labor, we strive, we play, we love, we seek. When our lives are prayerless all these are sometimes good, sometimes bad. But when our lives are full of prayer all else is made sublime. Our labors gain power and direction, our striving is after eternal victories, our playing is pure refreshment, our love becomes holy, and our seeking is after a glory that fadeth not away. Therefore we pray to thee.

Speak to each of us the word that he needs, and let that word abide in us until it has wrought in us thy holy will. Grant to each of us ears to hear what Simon heard, when Jesus said, "I have something to say *to you.*" Condemn our judgment of one another. As we forgive each other may we together seek thy forgiveness of our several faults. Being judged by thee separately, may we be forgiven by thee as one united people.

Our Father, we thank thee for the blessed joys of homecoming when old loves are quickened and old joys are lived again. We pray for all homes broken by enforced separation or by rancor or by death. Let the joys of happy homes be shared and also the sorrows of other homes. And hasten the day, we beseech thee, when all nations shall dwell together with thy world as their home and thee as their Father.

O God, as we return to the world of racing engines and blowing horns, of profits and losses, of hurrying and waiting, grant in thy mercy that we may carry from this place the peace which this noisy world can neither give nor take away. Let Sunday's seeds bring up a good harvest of righteousness in Monday's deeds. We pray in the name of him who lived upon the earth as the Prince of heaven, even Christ, thy Son. Amen.

Farewell Prayer

O *God,* thou art our God. We did not choose the place of our birth nor the family into which we were born. There is no skill or talent in us but thou didst put it there. All that we are, all that we have, all that we hope to become in days ahead, we owe to thee. Draw us close to thee in the miracle of worship, that in this hour we may know in surety that it is in thee we live and move and have our being.

O heavenly Father, who dost love us better than our own earthly parents or the dearest friends we have, increase daily our faith in thee. Help us to know in sorrow that without thee in our lives all is confusion and chaos and darkness. So shall we also know that when thou art by our side no street of life can be a blind alley or a dead end, for all our ways shall be thoroughfares leading sometimes through crooked and evil places, but always out again to the hills of personal victory in the sunlight of thy glory.

O God, we thank thee especially this day for this church, for the beloved community thou hast made of our fellowship as pastor and people. It has been good and in it we have had great joy. Sometimes we have learned hard lessons of sorrow together. More often we have been together happy laborers in thy vineyard. Now that this chapter in the history of our church is to end, grant us greatness of spirit sufficient to make the next chapter better than the last.

And go, we beseech thee, O God, with those who seek a new pastor for this church, that their choice may be thy choice and his coming thy call. In all things let our lives be not only strong but also joyful in continuing by labor and by prayer the tasks which thou dost give us to do. We offer all our prayers in the name of him who is the only Head of thy church, Jesus our Lord. Amen.

Index

150